ADVENTURES OF

1st Edition (rev 2)

Published in 2012 by
Woodfield Publishing Ltd
Bognor Regis PO21 5EL England
www.woodfieldpublishing.co.uk

ISBN 1-84683-129-6

Printed and bound in England

Cover design by Rowland Henry

Adventures of a Trenchard Brat

A former Royal Air Force Apprentice's experiences before, during and after World War II

KEN BARTROP
(44TH ENTRY, RAF HALTON)

Woodfield

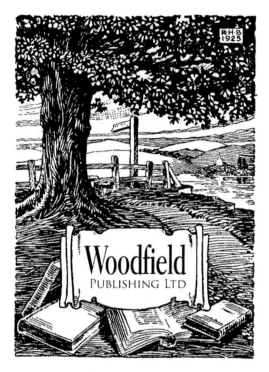

Woodfield Publishing Ltd

Bognor Regis ~ West Sussex ~ England ~ PO21 5EL
tel 01243 821234 ~ **e/m** info@woodfieldpublishing.co.uk

Interesting and informative books on a variety of subjects

For full details of all our published titles, visit our website at
www.woodfieldpublishing.co.uk

To Joan, Susan & Helen

~ CONTENTS ~

Preface.. *iii*

Introduction .... *iv*

1. Early Years.. 1
2. Unemployment... 11
3. Family Matters.. 15
4. The Learning Years 18
5. Secondary School 21
6. Wartime... 26
7. No.1 School of Technical Training............ 30
8. Man's Service 46
9. Destination Unknown............................... 48
10. India – Jewel of the East 55
11. Cawnpore.. 61
12. Homeward Bound 78
13. Kirton-in-Lindsey Again.......................... 84
14. Singapore Interlude................................. 89
15. Misemployment 93
16. Gliding Along 99
17. A Change of Direction............................. 104
18. Father-in-Law 105
19. Career Changes.. 107

20. RAF Habbaniyah 109

21. Life in the Desert 119

22. Bomber Command Development Unit....................127

23. Central Servicing Development Unit......................130

24. Education... 132

25. Return to Civilian Life 135

26. Living in France 140

27. My Parents 144

28. Joan's Parents 146

29. Extended Families 160

    Epilogue..164

Preface

I have dedicated this book to my dear wife Joan and our daughters, Susan and Helen. They had to put up with a lot as members of a Service family. Many times we were separated through lack of Married Quarters on many stations. Joan was never completely happy as a Service wife and deeply resented our periods of separation. Although I served in India, Singapore and Iraq and visited Cyprus and North Africa, she never was able to accompany me and, indeed, never left the United Kingdom until long after we left the RAF. When, after my tour as a Substitute Education Officer, which was probably the most satisfying job I ever had, I was offered the chance of a commission, Joan said she had had enough of the inevitable separation. I had to decide which was the more important, my career or a commission. I could always get another job, with my qualifications, but good marriages are very hard to repeat. So, I left the RAF and took a job in a High School, a move which I have regretted. The lack of discipline amongst today's youngsters makes teaching a very difficult job. That, coupled with a lot of back pain from an old injury, made me wonder if I should have stayed in the Service.

Introduction

I was infected with the 'aircraft virus' at an early age. A visit to a Flying Circus in the early 1930s instilled in me a love of aircraft which has continued throughout my life. Even though I left the Service more than forty-five years ago, I still have a strong interest in things, and people, aeronautical. I visit Air Museums and exhibitions and, when possible, fly in light aircraft such as Tiger Moths and Stearmans.

Almost all my friends are, or were, connected with the RAF. Each year, when possible, I join with other ex-apprentices at a hotel in Bournemouth for a reunion. As this involves a round trip of some 450 miles driving, I think I can call myself dedicated! Every third year we have a Triennial Reunion, so far at Halton, where around 3,000 former apprentices congregate to renew old memories.

Ex-apprentices, almost by definition, stick together and try to help each other. We all started as young boys and whilst a large proportion became aircrew and some reached the highest ranks in the Service, at reunions we are all, once more, equals.

1. Early Years

It was a glorious spring day and the little garden was ablaze with colour. On the lawn, two young boys were playing cricket. The younger blond one held the bat and looked belligerently at his older brother, who had just bowled him out for the second time. The older boy, a couple of years senior, stood, hands on hips, ball in hand, facing his brother.

"One more try and you're out. If you won't give me the bat I'll take the ball inside and you'll play by yourself."

With this, he turned, walked back to the bowling crease and bowled once more. The youngster waved his bat, missed the ball completely and saw his stumps fall once more. The older boy walked up to his brother, hand outstretched, and asked for the bat, which was refused yet again. Turning away, the older boy felt a heavy blow across the small of his back. His brother, in a fit of temper, had swung the bat and hit his playmate.

In spite of this incident, which could have had serious consequences, my brother and I grew up together and became quite good friends.

The house we lived in was in the north western suburbs of Sheffield, the time about 1932. It was, in fact, our parents' first proper house since their marriage in 1924. Dad was born in 1900 and lived, with his parents, in a terraced house in Pond Street in the centre of Sheffield. Mum was about six months older than her husband and had lived, with her parents, in a similar terraced house just round the corner in Turner Street. Both had been younger members of large families. Dad's parents had produced 14 children, though not all of these survived, whilst Mum had five sisters and two brothers, who all lived beyond the age of forty. Both of our parents left full- time education at the age of thirteen, when Mum went into service and Dad went to work in the steelworks.

The author as a young man.

World War 1 affected both their lives, as it did many others. They were both too young to see active service with the Armed Forces but my mother, eventually, found herself dismantling motorcycles in the Royal Flying Corps and, at the age of eighteen years, Dad was called up into the Army and sent to Germany in the Army of Occupation. He spent a year on a farm near Munich, I believe, and thoroughly enjoyed himself. On his return to civilian life he found himself, like many others of his age-group, out of work. It was to be almost sixteen years before he again found full employment. In the meantime, he found work wherever he could doing any job that was available.

After their marriage, at Saint Mary's Church, I believe my parents lived with relatives wherever they could be accommodated. Their first house to call their own was on a private housing development called The Sutton Estate. These houses, almost all semi-detached, were built on the side of a fairly steep hill some 2½ miles from the city centre. Our road, Colin Avenue, ran across the side of the hill so the houses on one side were built some five or six feet higher than the road surface, whilst their neighbours, opposite, were some feet below the road surface. No.9 was a two-bedroom semi-detached house in which lived Mum and Dad, Mum's younger brother Harry and we two boys. I had a bed in my parents' room whilst my brother, Dennis, shared Uncle Harry's room.

Uncle Harry was about three years younger than Mum and had always been a somewhat sickly child. On her deathbed, my grandmother asked her daughter to look after him and give him a roof over his head. My mother, who could always be relied upon to "go the extra yard", kept her promise and Harry lived with us well into the 1960s.

In those early days, my strongest memory is of Harry's singing. Sickly or not, he had a very good baritone voice, good enough to be a member of the Sheffield Philharmonic Choir. Between concerts, our house would ring to the sound of Harry rehearsing for the next performance in the City Hall. Few of his favourites seem to have survived until now, or, perhaps I have been listening to the wrong radio channels. I do remember a few of his songs. There was one about a blind man called Barty, and another told the tale of a crippled boy who walked up to a farmer's door to beg for work. *Who is Sylvia, What is she?* was another question frequently asked. There were many more but my memory is not what it used to be.

On concert nights there was a great deal of activity in the house. Harry had to get ready for his performance. Evening Dress was prepared in advance, by Mum of course, and she would help her brother into his finery. Cufflinks had to be inserted into shirtsleeves without creasing the sleeves. "Diamond" studs were fitted down the front of his shirt. Finally, there was the "Dicky-bow" to be arranged. When all was in place we would submit him to a thorough inspection to be sure of perfection. I never knew how he got from our front door to the City Hall, or, indeed, how he came home, but this whole exercise remains clear in my memory more than 75 years later.

As we progress through the 1930s, various things come to mind. On my 7th birthday, in 1933, I received a "fairy cycle" as a present. My first bike! My birthday was April 1st and we were on school holiday so I spent the whole of that morning learning to ride. There was no-one to help me but I persevered, growing redder and redder in the face, until I had mastered the art. There never was a prouder boy.

Later that year, we moved house to an almost new council house on the Wisewood Estate about 1½ miles from Colin Avenue. This house was one of the middle pair in a block of four. Again it had only two bedrooms but they were bigger and the position of the house was much more attractive.

Once again, Sheffield's hilly terrain dictated that our block of four houses, incidentally the last to be built on the estate, should be several feet above street level. In fact, we had to climb up eleven steps from the pavement to the level of the front garden and a further three steps to the front door. The small front garden was level from the house and retained from falling onto the pavement by a brick wall some six feet high, on top of which was a wrought iron fence.

Wisewood Estate was, and still is, a large Council Estate, having several hundred houses, two schools and quite a few shops around its boundaries. Our house was at the junction of Hallowmoor Road, which divides the estate roughly in two, and Wisewood Road, which forms the low-side boundary of the estate. At their junction, the two roads cross at an acute angle, so forming a very wide intersection. This wide space was to form our playground for some years to come. At that time there was very little traffic on the roads and we could play our games in safety. Travelling down the hill, the continuation of Hallowmoor Road was only a cinder track, six or seven feet wide, and this was made into a proper road several years later, to be known as Wisewood Lane. This eventually became part of a bus route connecting the estate to the City Centre.

The land on which the estate was built had been farmland and the old stone farmhouse had stood on the corner which now accommodated our home. It would seem that the builders had demolished the farmhouse and carried out only minimal clearance of the debris before building the final block of four houses. As a result of this, our gardens consisted of a thin layer of topsoil covering sizeable pieces of stone. The garden at Colin Avenue had been a far better proposition and my father had been able to make good use of the land to produce a supply of vegetables and a creditable display of flowers. Our house, being raised above the level of the road junction, had a magnificent view across the valley of the River Loxley and the uplands beyond. To the left rose the great hill of Crookes and Walkley whilst, swinging to the right, we could see Redmires, Stannington and Bradfield; in all a sweep of nearly ten miles. From the Victorian terrace houses of Crookes to the rolling hills of Bradfield Moors, there was always something to see.

As we boys settled into our new surroundings and made some new friends, we were still able to attend the same school as before and could, therefore, retain some of our old friends. We soon learned our way round the area and often strayed along the valley of the River Loxley, which flowed from the hills beyond Bradfield to join first the Rivelin and then the River Don. Along the Loxley valley were a number of factories of various types. The nearest of these were the twin factories of John Wood and Son, one of which produced steel billets and steel plates, whilst the other made wires and rods of various thicknesses. My brother and I soon discovered that our Uncle Fred, husband of Mum's sister Nellie, and their two sons Harry and Leslie and other members of our extended family, worked in the Rolling Mill. The entrance to this mill, only about a quarter of a mile from our house, was a gaping black hole perhaps fourteen feet high and twenty feet wide, through which we could see an occasional blaze of flames as a furnace door was opened, or showers of sparks accompanied by loud bangs as steam hammers shaped large lumps of steel into more manageable billets. At first, we would stand by the doorway, trying to make out what was happening, but before long we would stray into the workshop, eventually, right up to Uncle Fred's Hammer. These hammers were of different sizes according to the work on which they were employed. The smaller ones would strike more frequently with a "bonk, bonk, bonk" sound, whilst the larger ones, like the one Uncle Fred drove, would strike more slowly and deliberately with a much louder "BANG – BANG – BANG."

The heavy hammers were operated by teams of three men. One tended the furnace and brought the large blocks of white hot steel from the hearth to the hammer. A second man would help him, if necessary, but was mainly responsible for operating the hammer. He had control of the steam-valve which raised or lowered the bit which actually struck the work-piece. The third man, in our case Uncle Fred, was in overall charge of the proceedings. He sat on a seat, suspended from the roof of the building, and would swing to and fro, feeding the hot piece of metal under the hammer, turning it over from time to time until it was reduced to the required size. As the finished shape was approached the size of the item was checked with callipers until the finished size was achieved. Sometimes it was necessary to return the piece to the furnace for reheating.

Under today's Health and Safety Regulations we children would never be allowed through the door but in those "less-enlightened" days we were able to learn quite a lot about the process. We were able, also, to enjoy a further treat. Just to one side of the main entrance were the stables where the magnificent Shire horses were housed. These enormous animals seemed, to us, to be about fifteen feet high. In fact, they were probably nearer seven feet high, but we were only around 8 years old. If we were there at about four o'clock in the afternoon, the horses would have finished their day's work and the handler would sometimes let us ride on the animal's back. We would be hoisted up to the required height and struggle to straddle the broad backs of these docile creatures.

Further up the Loxley valley there were other steelworks, including one which had apparently been destroyed by a flood in the 19th century and, much higher up, there was a factory which produced sanitary wares, wash basins, toilets, etc. Each of these factories had a dam which drew water from the river, fed it into the factory where it was used in the various work processes and then returned it to the river.

The next dam in the valley was Dam Flask, so called because of its bottle-like shape. This formed a large part of the water supply for Sheffield and swimming was forbidden.

Still further on toward Strines Moor were two very large dams. One of these, named Dale Dyke Dam, whilst still under construction, burst its banks during the night of 11th March 1864, causing considerable damage and casualties. In all, 240 people were drowned, 100 buildings and 15 bridges were destroyed and 4,000 homes were flooded. Several people had miraculous escapes from death, perhaps none more so than a very young baby who was swept away in her cot. Some distance downstream her cot was caught up in reeds, where she was found. She was cared for by nurses in a nearby hospital and, since no trace of her parents was ever found, she was christened Mary Flood and survived to old age. On the dam between the two John Wood factories, Mr Wood's son kept a small yacht and, on more than one occasion, took me for a sail round the dam.

We boys enjoyed ourselves with simple games, making our own rules and various pieces of equipment as we went along. One of our favourite pastimes involved finding a patch of yellow clay, a fairly easy task alongside the Loxley valley. We would mould the clay to make Touch Burners. These were, essentially, narrow boxes, like very small coffins in shape, with removable lids. We would spend some time working the clay into flat strips, perhaps one and a half inches wide and four or five inches long. Three of these strips would be stuck together and the ends blocked off to form a box. The lid would be detachable, for reasons which will become clear. When we were satisfied with our efforts and the fit of their lids, they would be hidden away in a convenient hole. After a day, or so, the clay would have hardened and the box would be ready to receive its contents. This would be the start of a serious search for rotten wood from one of the trees which had been felled by wind or some other force. There was never a shortage of this so-called "touchwood" as there were numbers of trees nearby and many which had suffered the rigours of rough weather. This wood got its name from its texture; it almost literally fell to pieces at the touch of a hand. We would break the wood into small pieces and, with a little paper as kindling, we would create a fire in our boxes. Gradually, the heat of the fire would bake the clay until it became hard enough to withstand fairly rough treatment. By carefully positioning the lid, to control the ventilation, the fire would burn very slowly and we would try to keep our burner going as long as possible. A simple game but in several ways educational, in that we learned to find and work the clay, construct the box and carefully manage the fire to economise the fuel and control the burning rate.

We had to learn to amuse ourselves, especially in the long summer holidays, with a minimum of equipment. None of our families could be classified as even remotely well off. Most of our fathers worked in the various steelworks in the area. Some were machine operators, some blacksmiths or cutlers, but all had one thing in common, poverty. We lads were all lucky enough to be well fed, reasonably well clothed and fairly healthy and ready to turn our hands to different things to amuse ourselves. I cannot remember ever hearing a lad complain of boredom.

Football, cricket and swimming were probably our favourite pastimes and there was always fierce rivalry between the different groups. On the opposite side of the river to our homes, there was a group of allotments adjacent to the football and cricket grounds belonging to the steel works of John Wood. We would make friends with the men who tended these allotments and would often give a hand. In return we might be rewarded with an apple or two or a bunch of flowers for Mum.

Another thing which interested us was a couple of men who brought along greyhounds to train them for racing. The dogs were quite young and seemed to know less about racing than we did. The men had an old bicycle frame with only one wheel, and that had no tyre. Instead, a long length of cord was wound round the rim of the wheel and was attached to a rabbit's skin at the end of the cord. One man would draw out the cord to its full extent and then take one of the dogs a little further away. His partner would then turn the bicycle pedals to wind in the cord and the first man would release the dog who would try to catch the rabbit. Needless to say, we soon found ourselves volunteering to turn the pedals. All quite harmless fun and we kept ourselves out of mischief.

2. Unemployment

At this time, my Dad was having a great deal of trouble finding work. Sheffield, at the beginning of the 1930s, was about as grey and depressing as any city can be. The whole atmosphere of the place seemed full of despair. On every street corner shabby, unkempt men gathered to share a smoke and to mutter about the trouble. Crouched on their haunches, they would pass the cigarette from one to another, each one taking a draw before surrendering it to his neighbour. Each would hold the cigarette between thumb and the first two fingers with the lighted end sheltered towards the palm of his hand. In this way, the cigarette was protected from any passing breeze which might accelerate the burning of the precious tobacco.

From time to time a few souls, luckier than their friends, would play a game called Pitch and Toss, in which coins were tossed against a wall by each man in turn. A coin which covered another would be declared a winner and its owner would retrieve both coins. A close watch had to be kept for the police because such gambling was illegal.

Most of these men had known better times; times when they did not need to share their cigarettes; times when they did not have to hang about on street corners. Many of them had worked for years in the steelworks which had made their city famous throughout the world. The recent World War had kept their factories busy for twenty-four hours a day. Now, in peace time there was little call for their skills. Many of the younger ones had never known work. They had left school at the age of thirteen or fourteen years, and had joined the queue of jobless at the Labour Exchange. This was "The Trouble" which occupied so much of their time and conversation. Eighteen per cent of the work force was unemployed. There were so many unemployed men in the city that the Labour Exchange could deal with only a section of them each day. Surnames starting with A to D would report on Monday; the E's to H on Tuesday, and so on... Outside the Exchange, every morning, long queues of men would form long before the time of opening. By nine o'clock, the usual opening time, the streets would be jammed by masses of soulless men. Queues were surprisingly orderly. But then, nobody wanted to draw attention to the fact that they were there. Most were ashamed that they had to beg for work in this undignified manner, and even more ashamed that they had to beg for the "dole," the pittance that the Government would pay as Unemployment Benefit.

The womenfolk had their problems too. With their husbands out of work, wives had to manage to feed their husbands, themselves and, perhaps, two or more children. Clothes had to be cared for, especially the husband's best suit, in case he should be lucky enough to be called for an interview. On their shopping trips, women would plan their routes to avoid any chance of passing the Labour Exchange where their men were queuing, especially if they had been obliged to take their children with them. The children must not be allowed to see their fathers in the undignified role of beggars-for-work.

Later, after the few available jobs had been filled and the last pittance paid out, those same men could be seen meandering home, aimlessly, dejectedly, many with tears in their eyes and lead in their hearts.

For several years, my father had been one of these jobless men but one day it seemed things may be about to change. Through the grapevine, in the person of Charlie, his old foreman, Dad heard that his old firm were "setting on". It appeared they wanted to interview certain former employees and Dad was one of them.

On the day, Dad made himself as presentable as possible, dressed me in my best clothes and off we went. I have never found out why he took me along on that day. I could not have been more than seven or eight years old at the time. Perhaps he needed my moral support. Perhaps the sight of me was supposed to soften the manager's heart and secure the job. Whatever the reason, I was taken along and, young as I was, certain events of that day have stayed in my memory ever since. Much of the detail of the day has long since left me but I have a very clear picture in my mind of the machine-shop and of my father's face.

The day was fine and the sun shone down from a cloudless sky. As we entered the factory I could see long rows of machines stretching down the factory floor, and, overhead, I remember the maze of shafts, belts and pulleys which, I now know, provided the driving power for these machines. The slanting rays of sunshine through the window showed the myriad motes of dust, no doubt stirred up by our passage. None of the machines appeared to be working for I could see, quite clearly, the thin film of reddish-brown rust over everything. I remember we crossed the shop floor to look at Dad's machine. It, too, was covered in rust.

I remember looking at my father's face as he regarded that rusting pile of metal. Tears were coursing down his cheeks. I realised, even then, that he loved his work and his machine. The thought, and sight, of his beloved lathe rusting away was too much for him. He was crying! I had never seen a man cry before and I never saw my father cry again after that day. The memory will always be with me. Here was a man who loved his work, who wanted to work, but for whom there was to be no work, or at least regular work, for some time to come. I was but a child and he was my father. There must have been thousands of others like him who desperately wanted to work, who needed to work to give them the right to be men once more.

In the mid-30s there came the troubles in Germany. I was too young, at the time, to understand what exactly was going on. I cannot be certain whether my father was successful in his quest for work, accompanied by me, his eldest son, but I do know that, about 1935, he went back to work at his old firm. There was much talk about re-armament, whatever that was, and, it seems, my family's life took a change for the better.

3. Family Matters

By some strange coincidence, this was about the time my second brother arrived, though not without a certain amount of trouble. My mother was admitted to hospital leaving Dad to care for his two boys as well as working shift work. During the week, it was arranged that my brother and I would be cared for by Aunty Nellie, who lived only about 200 yards away, but on Friday afternoon I would catch the bus into Sheffield when school was over, then take another bus to Mosborough, about eight miles south-east of the city, where I would spend the weekend with Auntie Florrie, one of Mum's elder sisters. This went on for some seven or eight weeks prior to the Easter Holidays, when I stayed for ten days. I vaguely knew that Mum was not well and had been taken into hospital. Much later, I learned that she suffered, what was called a White Leg. This was a fairly serious complication in her pregnancy but, of course, this was the thirties and such things were not discussed in front of nine-year-old boys. Indeed, I did not know I was to have another brother until I was introduced to him, in his cot, some days later.

There were plenty of fields within easy reach of our home and we often played football with groups of friends. I should say that football was our favourite sport, though we all seemed to enjoy swimming, whether in the various dams and reservoirs or at the local swimming baths. Cycling was a very popular pastime and, from the age of about eleven years, we, my brother and I, and our friend Ronnie Wilson, would ride out on a Sunday morning to explore Derbyshire and the Peak District. I suppose we might cover anything from 30 to 50 miles visiting Baslow, Hathersage, Bakewell, Tideswell, Eyam, Castleton and many other villages. We never seemed to tire of the area with its hills, valleys, forests and inspiring buildings. On more than one occasion we visited Chatsworth House, the home of the Duke and Duchess of Devonshire, where we would marvel at the paintings of a pair of partridges on a door or , on another door, a painting of a violin. They looked so real.

Perhaps some of this interest filtered down from Uncle Harry. When his health would allow, he would put a piece of bread and cheese in his pocket and explore a similar area on foot. Where we would cycle along the lanes, Harry would strike out, cross-country, over Kinder Scout or Mam Tor. Once, when the family was away at Trusthorpe or Sutton-on-Sea, just south of Mablethorpe in Lincolnshire, Harry was taken ill and rushed into Sheffield Infirmary. We later heard that he had been diagnosed with a tumour on his spine. His future looked rather bleak; the doctors said that if the tumour continued to grow it would crush his spine and if it burst it would poison his system. There was nothing they could do to alleviate this situation except to prescribe painkillers. The family, Mum, Dad, Dennis and I, along with Auntie Nellie, Uncle Fred, their two sons, two daughters, each with their boy or girl friend, were in a holiday resort some 90 miles away. Things had not been plain sailing for us. One of the young couples had an altercation with a bus in Louth High Street and, though not seriously hurt were taken into hospital for observation. Their motorcycle was not seriously damaged. Also, whilst playing cricket outside our accommodation, Dennis was stung on his knee by a wasp, which caused his knee to double in size.

Harry was in hospital for some time and, in spite of all contrary forecasts, made a very good recovery. As soon as he felt strong enough, he resumed his survey of the Peak District and gradually rebuilt his physique. In 1939, when the war started, he was working in Hadfield's Steel Works on a large furnace making 60 tons of steel at a time. With many of his friends in the Armed Forces, Harry thought he was missing out on the adventure, so he applied to join the Royal Navy as a stoker. He thought his furnace-tending experience would stand him in good stead and guarantee his place afloat. Of course, a medical certificate was required, so, undaunted, he went to see his doctor. Dr McPhail had been our family doctor for many years and knew Harry's history very well. Harry's body-building had been so successful that when he walked into the consulting room and gave his name, the poor doctor could not believe his eyes. After a look at Harry's record, the doctor sat down heavily and said one word, "Impossible!" He could not believe what he could see in front of him but after a thorough examination he had to confess that his patient was 'Fit for Anything'. However, Harry was in for a disappointment, since his position in the steelworks was deemed "Work of National Importance" and so he spent the whole of World War II working shifts to produce hundreds of tons of steel. On several occasions he sent home a message that he would be working a double shift. The work was so heavy and in such harsh conditions that occasionally a man would collapse and, if unfortunate enough, fall into the ladle of molten steel. In such circumstances Harry, being a single man, felt it his duty to stand in for the casualty.

4. The Learning Years

The 1930s was to be a very important influence in my life for it was at that time that I was introduced to aeroplanes. There were at that time a few intrepid individuals who toured the country demonstrating their skills in what became known as 'Flying Circuses'. They would bring their machines to a suitable field on the outskirts of the city and, making a small charge to cover expenses, would put on flying displays. The most popular planes were de Havilland Tiger Moths and Hawker Harts or Hinds. Occasionally we might see a Sopwith Pup or a Bristol Fighter, though these were not so common. All of these were biplanes and would fly in formations, perform aerobatics or demonstrate their use as mail collection and delivery vehicles. Some aircraft had a small platform fitted to the central part of the upper wing. A young lady, scantily dressed, would stand on the platform doing simple exercises in flight to the delight of the spectators. Other aircraft had a metal hook attached underneath and would fly very low to pick up sacks of mail which would be delivered and released further down the flight path. That may seem very tame compared to today's displays by the Red Arrows and their like, but this was really in the infancy of flying and crowds were fascinated by what they saw.

Not least entranced was Yours Truly. I decided, there and then that I wanted to spend my life working on flying machines. Strangely, perhaps, I was not particularly drawn to actually flying the planes but I was fascinated by their engines. I wanted to work on aircraft engines.

I became very interested in the construction of aircraft when someone bought me a Christmas present of a flying model aircraft. It came in a box, about the size of a shoebox, in which were the fuselage, two wings and the winding mechanism for energising the "motor" (an elastic band) which was stretched from the propeller to the tail end of the craft. My brother, Dennis, also had one of these wonderful machines and we persuaded Dad to take us down to Hillsborough Park on Christmas afternoon where we learned to fly our craft. Later, I was given a Meccano Aircraft Construction Kit, consisting of all the parts required to make two different planes using nuts and bolts and metal panels supplied in the kit. I spent many happy hours with both presents. I even borrowed a book from the local library called *How To Build An Aeroplane*. This was really an instruction manual detailing the building of a high wing monoplane, something like a Cessna, from scratch. Needless to say, this was far in advance of my very basic skills, or, indeed, understanding, but I ploughed through it to the bitter end.

In 1936, at the age of ten, I was offered a place at Marlcliffe Road Intermediate School. My parents were persuaded that I should not accept the place but should spend a year in the senior department of Wisewood School, then, hopefully, qualify for a better school. I am firmly convinced that this was a very wise decision. I had been quite happy in the junior department of Wisewood School but in the seniors I came under the influence of some very special teachers. In fact, I think most, if not all, of those members of staff were very good but two stand out in my memory. Winifred Handley was my Form teacher and taught me English. At the end of many lessons she would divide the class into two groups on either side of the classroom. We would then, in turn, ask our opposite number to spell a word. If the answer was correct, the team gained a point but if the answer was wrong and the questioner could spell it correctly, then his team gained the point. I am sure that by this method I became a much better and more confident speller. Miss Handley also encouraged me to write good English, a skill which has stood me in good stead throughout my life.

Elisabeth Fielden was my mathematics teacher and also taught me the rudiments of technical drawing. She taught me the basics of arithmetic and, I believe, if she could have been my teacher for a year or two longer, I may have done even better in my later education.

In September 1937 I moved on to Firth Park Secondary School for Boys, which was reckoned to be the third best school in Sheffield. My time there commenced in September 1937 and, since my parents were not in a financial position to support me there, I was granted a scholarship by the Sheffield Education Committee, on condition that I stayed in full-time education until, at least, my sixteenth birthday. This was readily agreed at the time but was to be the cause of some discussion later.

5. Secondary School

The first day at Firth Park was naturally, I suppose, somewhat daunting. From the new buildings of the Wisewood Schools, with their quite large adjacent playgrounds to the much higher, older buildings of the new school, was a big contrast. The new school was a boys-only school and there were 600 of us.

Luckily, I had arrived at the school by bus along with several friends from my old school, so I was not quite as isolated as might have been expected. Soon after our arrival, a bell rang and the milling throng sorted itself into long parallel lines, each line containing the boys of one particular class, or 'Form', as we were now to be known. The new boys were, of course, not yet allocated a Form, so we lined up behind everybody else. The old hands marched into the Assembly Hall for morning prayers and the process of sorting the newcomers began.

For want of a better system, our names had been listed in order of the results of the Entrance Exam so, naturally, I came about one third of the way down the list of the lowest form, Form 1D. Our form room was on the upper floor of a comparatively new building and our Form Master was Mr A E Wetherill, a tall man with thinning hair and a sense of humour. In addition to being our Form teacher, he also taught us French and, on alternate Wednesdays, took us over to the playing field for football.

During that first year we learned the usual subjects geography, history, English, mathematics, physics, chemistry, metalwork and, of course, physical training.

All of our teachers were specialists in their own particular subject and almost all had some habit or peculiarity which made them unique. Norman Frost, our music teacher, was a tall, slim man with an anxious look on his face. This was, no doubt, a result of preparing a School Choir, of some three hundred boys, to put on a concert in the City Hall each November. This concert was broadcast live on the BBC Home Service. Remarkable when one considers that, of the three hundred, at least one third had only been at the school for two-and-a-half months and the programme was quite ambitious. I well remember our first experience when we sang several songs which included "Who is Sylvia?" and "Ombra Mai Fu" which we learned phonetically in the original language. The programme usually included one or two soloists, some professionals and other senior members of the school who showed ability. The concerts had been a tradition of the school for some time and were well supported by the citizens of Sheffield.

Other members of staff who were distinguished included Mr Carr, the Art teacher, who was unfortunate in having a very pronounced limp, hence his nickname of 'Hoppy'. He must have been well past the retiring age when I joined the school and held his post on the staff, I believe, throughout the Second World War. He taught me Art and the History of Art for three years and I never remember him referring to notes. Throughout the lesson, Hoppy would lean against his desk or take a walk round the classroom, his tutoring covering at least five hundred years of Art and artists without pause for thought. He was phenomenal.

Bill Sedgewick, my maths teacher, was less than half the age of Hoppy, a fit and active young man who delighted in telling me what a wonderful example I was to my younger brothers. His sarcasm was rather hurtful but he was right. Maths was never my best subject although, for my sins, no doubt, I taught the subject for several years later in life. After the Summer Holidays, it must have been September 1940, I think, Mr Sedgewick did not return to school. At morning assembly the Headmaster, Mr Padfield, announced that Bill had died during a Home Guard Exercise.

My English teacher was Dr F T Wood, a very quiet, studious kind of man, said to be the most highly academically qualified in the school.

I feel I must mention one more member of staff, although he was only there for one year of my time at the school. His name was Jack Bridge and he taught physics, having joined us, I believe, straight from college. He was a good teacher and quite popular. Soon after he joined us, he read an advertisement asking for volunteers for secret, dangerous work. He soon found himself in a Naval Officer's uniform, learning how to neutralise unexploded armaments in dockyards and on vessels. In a varied career throughout Europe, he was awarded a George Cross and two George Medals, the highest awards for ' bravery when not in direct contact with the enemy'. He survived the war and re-turned to teach at Firth Park after demobilisation.

Incidentally, Jack Bridge's place in school was filled by a cer-tain Harry Wrather, who deserves a mention. He was of stocky build and medium height and had some interesting hobbies. In an area almost entirely devoted to soccer, he played rugby for Sheffield Tigers. He tried, I believe, to introduce rugby to the school but with little success. His other hobby was photography and I was lucky enough to see a film he brought to school. It was beautifully made and entitled "A Year in the Life of a Fox". It ran for about an hour and was, I feel sure, of professional standard.

The beginning of the war in 1939 coincided with the start of my third year at Firth Park. This was to be an important time in my school life. Although I had started in the D form in my first year, by the second year I had progressed to the B stream. This meant that my progress would be accelerated and I would sit my School Certificate Exam in the fourth rather than fifth year.

When the war started, all schools were closed until Air Raid Shelters had been created sufficient to house the whole school's population. Earth moving equipment was brought in and workmen proceeded to tear up our sports field alongside the road outside the school. A long zig-zag trench was dug, about seven feet deep, lined with concrete and similarly roofed over. The whole procedure took almost six months to complete. Meanwhile, emergency classes were arranged. Since the population of the school was drawn from all over the Sheffield district, the classes had to be similarly spread out. Parents were asked to volunteer the use of a room, if big enough to accommodate about ten boys, where a teacher could meet a group and issue them with worksheets.

Each group might contain boys of different ability and interest and the teacher might be of a specialism not covered by the boys in the group. The group to which I was allocated met in a large house about two miles from my home. We would meet there two or three times a week when the teacher would collect work for marking and issue work sheets for various subjects. The teacher would supervise us for an hour or two, giving help where his specialism was suitable. In many cases there would be boys in the group who could help younger ones with their work. It seems to be fairly complicated but seemed to work quite well.

During the war, both in and out of school, people co-operated with each other to a much greater extent than is common today. Schoolboys were not averse to helping each other. The language lessons were very interesting, since, in any of the groups, there might be boys studying one or more of the four languages taught in the school. I, for example, was studying French and German but in my group there were boys studying Spanish and Italian. Fortunately, there are similarities between these languages and we were able to learn bits of each other's tongues. This haphazard form of education went on for the whole six-month period whilst the shelters were being constructed. On our return to school, there was a lot of catching up to be done.

Eventually the air-raid shelters were finished and we were able to resume our school life in the proper surroundings. Naturally, we boys wanted to see what had been holding us up for so long and tours of inspection were arranged in the form of air-raid drills. Although we often saw huge flights of aircraft flying overhead, apparently on their way to another raid on German or Norwegian targets, we were never called upon to occupy the shelters 'in earnest', so to speak.

Life went on as normally as possible and thoughts of examinations began to form in our minds. Normally, in the summer holidays of our third year at the school we would have been offered the opportunity to take part in an exchange programme with a Boys' School in Germany. Such trips had been a feature of the curriculum for some time. Unfortunately, such goings-on were cancelled out by the war, so we were robbed of the opportunity to practice our language skills and see how the other half lived. It was to be almost forty-five years before I was able to speak to a German person – but that's the way life goes sometimes.

6. Wartime

Many of my friends, like me, took on new activities as a contribution to the War Effort. The first thing I took on was to act as a casualty so that First Aiders could learn to deal with live patients. During the light evenings we would report to one of the local schools and, after a briefing, as to the extent of our 'injuries', we would lie on a stretcher and people would come along and try to diagnose our ailments before splinting and bandaging our 'broken legs', 'fractured skulls', 'ruptured spleens' and the like. By carefully watching these trainees, we learned quite a lot of techniques that might prove useful later on the street after an air raid or on the football pitch. Another of my voluntary jobs was as a courier for the Ministry of Information. This important sounding job was, in fact, quite important. After an air raid, communications might be destroyed, people would be displaced if their homes had been damaged or demolished and someone must gather information and report it to a central office.

Our job, as couriers, would be to go to the scene of a bombing, find out who was injured or homeless and relay this to the central office in the City Library. We wore an armband with the logo MOI (Ministry of Information) and travelled around on our bicycles. My worst experience on this duty was when my incident proved to be at the home of a classmate. He was safe and his parents lightly injured, but his teenage sister had been killed. Travelling round the city after a heavy raid could be rather nerve-wracking at times, since the authorities may not have had time to clear up and there may be bodies or body parts in the street. After one very heavy raid, a German aircraft had crashed on the wreckage of a city centre pub and was plainly visible from a nearby road, with its pilot, still seated in the burned out cockpit, silhouetted against the sky.

I still had the burning desire to work on aircraft, but how to bring it about? A cousin, whose husband had been called up in the Naval Reserve and was left to run a fairly large public house in one of the better districts of Sheffield, asked me to help with the clearing up at the weekend. I agreed and would go there on Saturday afternoon to help prepare the ballroom for the usual Saturday dance. On Sunday morning, my real duties commenced as I swept out the ballroom, cleared up all the glasses, etc, then outside to clean out the toilets and clear any obstructions from pathways. Sometimes I might be invited to stay for a few days, if it was during the school holidays and, on one of these occasions my cousin had provided facilities for a meeting of Senior RAF Officers.

"Here Ken," she said. "You want to join the Air Force, don't you? Why not ask these chaps how's the best way to go about it?" I was extremely shy at that time but Doris practically dragged me into the room to meet her guests. They were very pleasant and said the best plan was to apply to join the service as an Aircraft Apprentice at Halton. I had never heard of Halton, or Aircraft Apprentices, but I went along to the RAF Recruiting Office and got all the information. First, I was under the age of sixteen so I must have parental consent. Then, I must take a written exam in English, Maths and General Knowledge. If I passed, I would go to Halton in Buckinghamshire and, after passing a stringent medical exam, I would be accepted to sign on for twelve years from the age of eighteen.

There were three of us, candidates for the exam, in Sheffield and we had to report to a school in the city centre. By some strange coincidence, one of the candidates was Don Small. We had attended the same church for some time and had walked our girlfriends together, after services, on several occasions but the subject of joining the RAF had never been mentioned. Neither of us knew that the other one was interested in the Service. The third candidate went to the same school as Don, so they knew each other also. When the exam was over, we went our separate ways and waited for the results.

On the morning of February 9th 1942, a letter, addressed to me, dropped on the doormat as I was having breakfast. It looked very official and contained my Calling Up papers, official forms from the Air Ministry, requiring me to report for duty at RAF Halton on Wednesday 18th February 1942. I went off to school with a light step, expecting to tell the Headmaster about my letter but, to my surprise, he knew already and passed on the news to the whole assembled school.

"I have to tell you that Bartrop, of Mr Wetherill's Form, has been accepted by the Royal Air Force as a trainee apprentice. He passed an entrance examination... Was that a competitive exam, Bartrop, and was it open to all-comers?"

"Yes, Sir. It was competitive and was open to all British boys."

"Congratulations, Bartrop. I have to tell you that before he sat the test I told Bartrop that I did not think he would Pass. I was wrong."

That day, a Thursday, and the following day, passed rather quickly as I had to hand in all my textbooks to the teachers who had issued them. There were a few other things to be dealt with and, finally, I left school for the last time and caught the bus for home. I had decided to have the next ten days as a sort of holiday when I could say my goodbyes to friends and relations. However, it was not to be the quiet few days that I had intended. When Sheffield Education Committee checked their records, they realised that Mr & Mrs Bartrop had signed an agreement that their son would remain at school until, at least, his sixteenth birthday, six weeks ahead. After much to-ing and fro-ing they realised that there was a war in progress and the boy in question had received his Mobilisation Papers. There was no question but he must report, as directed, or be arrested for desertion. That was the law and it must be obeyed. In any case, he was going into full-time education.

Dad was very busy with his work and did not say much but I have a sneaking suspicion that he was just a little bit proud to have a son in the RAF.

7. No.1 School of Technical Training

Wednesday 18th February 1942 started very fresh and fine. A watery sun shone through a light mist as we gathered on No.3 Platform of the LNER station for the 0755 train to London. There were not many passengers for that train and it was easy to identify the three groups of parents seeing off their sons. On the platform the groups were separated but, as the train moved out, we shared a compartment. Conversation was sparse at first, as, I suppose, we had our private thoughts about our unknown futures. One thing we all knew was that if we passed the stringent medical exam, our initial engagement would be for "12 years from the age of 18 years". That seemed a long time, especially as two of us had not yet celebrated our 16th birthdays and the third member of our group was only just 16.

Watching the scenery flash by as the train chugged its way south towards Nottingham, Loughborough, Leicester and all points leading to Kings Cross, we gradually opened up and began to talk to each other. I don't recall any specific subjects we discussed but we gradually got to know a bit more about each other. Surprisingly, we each had a fairly clear idea of what we would like to do in the Service. Don had ideas about being an Instrument Fitter and we had a few cracks about what kinds of instruments they might be. I, of course, was firmly fixed on a career with aircraft engines as an Engine Fitter, whilst Bob Oversby, the third member of our group, was all set to be an

Airframe Fitter. At this rate, we could almost start our own Air Force.

All too soon the train was winding its way through the London suburbs and into Kings Cross Station. We did not have a great deal of luggage, since, if we passed the medical exam, we would be parcelling our civilian clothes to send them home in a day or two. Gathering ourselves together, we left the train and made our way to the Underground Station. My only previous trip to London had been a school trip to do Country Dancing at Wembley Stadium in a Festival of Youth to celebrate the Coronation of King George VI in 1936, so I allowed myself to be guided to Baker Street and the Metropolitan Line, where we were to meet all the other youngsters who would be our classmates for the next two years.

Quite a few had arrived before us and, no doubt, there would be many more before our train arrived. We learned that there would be about three hundred of us so a 'special' train had been provided. By mid-afternoon the platform was packed and, at long last, the train arrived and we were all aboard. The Guard blew his whistle and the train pulled away from the platform. We were on our way to stations whose names we would learn to recite like a litany, Harrow-on-the-Hill, Rickmansworth, Chorley Wood, Amersham, Great Missenden and, finally, Wendover, the nearest station to RAF Halton. From here, we were loaded into lorries for the last 1½ miles of our journey.

The lorries stopped alongside a parade ground of tarmac perhaps a hundred yards square. Along one side of this we could see the administrative and medical offices and a flagpole flanked by two ancient guns. On two other sides were groups of red brick buildings, the barrack blocks, six on each side in three pairs. These were our first impressions of the camp which was overlooked by the Chiltern Hills. We were aware of other buildings whose purpose was not quite so obvious. We later found these were the cookhouse, a small gymnasium and the NAAFI canteen, a most important place, where we might be able to supplement our meals. Soon after our arrival we were separated into groups of about twenty-four and taken to our temporary quarters for the night. Each group were taken into a room lined with beds known as 'McDonalds'. Not the McDonalds which we now see on almost every street corner around the world, these were called McDonalds because they gave nothing! Above each bed, and secured to the wall, was a steel cupboard in which we would learn to display our kit, should we pass the fitness tests and be accepted. Each room was supervised by a NCO Apprentice who showed his new charges where they could find washbasins, toilets, etc, in an area called 'Ablutions'. These young boys would also tell us our timetable for the following day and where and when we would be fed. Having travelled nearly all day, we were ready to try our first RAF meal. I have always had a healthy appetite and I was ready to eat anything, which is just as well because my first meal was to be Cheese and Potato Pie. Just about the only food I hated was cheese, but I cleared my plate in good time.

After the meal we made our way back to the barrack room and spent some time getting to know each other. Soon enough the clock moved round and it was nearly time for "Lights Out" at half past nine. Most of us had a last splash in the sink, cleaned our teeth and returned to our beds. At exactly nine thirty the NCO Apprentice made sure we were all present and then switched off the lights. After a very short period of light conversation we settled down to sleep. Soon the room was almost silent, except for the soft sound of crying. Fifteen or sixteen years of age is not the easiest time to leave home for a totally new way of life. Gentle snores soon drowned any other sounds and the new entry slept.

Morning arrived to the sound of a trumpeter sounding Reveille at six thirty hours. As new arrivals we were excused the early morning Physical Training which was to be the normal start to the day's activities, so we washed and dressed in comparative comfort and prepared for breakfast. The RAF, it seemed were firm believers in a good start to the day with a choice of porridge or cereals, followed by a Full English breakfast with a choice of eggs, bacon, tomato, baked beans, etc, accompanied by toast.

Those first few days were quite an eye-opener for most of us. After breakfast we were taken, in groups, to the Medical Services block, otherwise known as Sick Bay, where we were told to undress, completely, and make ready for our medical examination. There we were, dozens of naked teenagers, queuing in the corridors whilst lots of young members of the Women's Royal Air Force passed to and fro, causing a great deal of embarrassment. Most of these girls were only two or three years older than us but they, no doubt, had seen it all before. We soon discovered that one of the Medical Officers was a rather gorgeous blonde of about twenty-five years and she would examine and question us about our medical history in the close proximity of a consulting room. More than one boy found himself aroused by her nearness and was dealt a sharp blow on the offending member with a pencil. I can only remember one candidate being rejected on medical grounds and he was failed by a set of teeth that were so bad as to jeopardise his future health. For those who were accepted, the next step was to take the Solemn Oath of Loyalty. Crowded into a small room, we were told the meaning of the oath and an Officer read out certain sections from the book of the King's Regulations for the Royal Air Force, otherwise known as 'King's Regs'. This done, we raised our right arms, stood to attention, and, after the Officer had read out the oath, we replied, "I do." That was that; we were in!

Next stop, the Barber's Shop and our first regulation haircut. I thought I had been given a "short back and sides" before I left home but that barber still found plenty to cut off. No wonder he was always referred to as Sweeney Todd. Some of the lads had taken a real pride in their hairstyles and some left the shop in tears. We did not have much time to cry over our lost locks as we prepared for our next encounter with authority at the clothing stores. Here we were kitted out with Working Dress, Parade Dress, Underwear, Towels, Sports Kit, Boots and all the other paraphernalia of Service Life. Very little regard was paid to size so there was a fair amount of swapping with someone else who had been given ill-fitting garments. Only impossibly badly fitting garments would be exchanged by the storeman. All items of kit had to be marked with the recipient's number, rank and name and we were made to understand that we were personally responsible for its upkeep and cleanliness. From that moment on we were to wear uniform at all times and, on that day, we had to parcel up our civilian clothing and send it home, postage paid by the RAF. I don't believe many of us realized that we had worn civilian clothes for the last time for almost fifteen years. We were still growing, at the age of sixteen years, or thereabouts, clothing was rationed and would remain so until the early fifties.

Those first few days at Halton were at the start of a very steep learning curve for all of us, but there was little time for feeling depressed. Almost every minute of every day was occupied by some activity. Some groups of our Entry started learning their new trades immediately, whilst others started learning the intricacies of the parade ground. I was in one of these latter groups and we spent the first six weeks of our training learning all about marching, saluting, dressing at the halt, in quick time, slow time, slow marching, in line abreast and column of route, and the drill for ceremonial occasions. I had been a member of the Church Lads Brigade so I had some idea what was expected, but many of my colleagues had to learn from the very beginning. Discipline was very strict but fair. After all, self-discipline is extremely important and is, probably, best learned from communal discipline. Members of a fighting force must learn to react instinctively to developing situations and play their part as members of a team.

As apprentices we were paid one shilling (5p) per day. Pay parades were held on alternate Thursdays when we received seven shillings (35p), the remainder of our entitlement, known as 'deferred pay' or 'credits', was kept in account to cover any breakages or losses of equipment, and the balance to be paid before we went on leave. Six weeks after our arrival at Halton was my birthday, April 1st, and was also the first day of our Easter leave. Another happy coincidence was that from that day we received a fifty per cent pay rise, the first rise since the Apprentice Scheme started in 1922, and the only rise throughout our two-year course.

Arrangements for our leave travel were made by the authorities. Our only involvement was to march the one-and-a-half miles to Wendover station, led by the Pipe Band. Trains which would normally run straight through this little station would stop to pick up happy boys going home to see their mums. Our Easter leave lasted ten days then we were back to camp until the three-week break of the summer holiday, which would start in July. I must confess that I found it very strange to be marching round Sheffield in a shiny new RAF uniform, including a 'cheese-cutter', the peaked hat with a green band to signify membership of No.1 Wing, RAF Halton. To the best of my knowledge, the three of us, Don Small, Bob Oversby and I were the only people so dressed in Sheffield.

The holiday spell passed all too quickly and we were, once again, on that platform waiting for the train to Wendover. The group to which I belonged now commenced our Workshop Phase of training. I was a member of a group of ten boys allocated to the charge of an elderly gentleman by the name of Mr Tatem. Much later, we learned that his given name was Harry and we always used that name amongst ourselves. Harry was one of the original members of the RAF when it was formed from the Royal Flying Corps, soon after the end of the First World War. I believe his Service Number (the serial number by which he was recognised officially) was 253. He was a very friendly, gentle man as well as being an excellent tradesman and instructor. His job was to teach us the basic skills of using engineering tools. We learned to use files, chisels, hammers, etc. and to weld and solder, so that we could make, or attempt to make any spare part which may be required to repair any mechanism we might come across.

At that time, most aircraft were made of aluminium, but we were also taught to work with copper, steel, brass and cast iron. Precision was the keynote of our work and the tasks set involved working to limits quoted in thousands of an inch. To this end, we had to learn to use micrometers, Vernier callipers, surface tables and other precision instruments. Sheet metals were on the syllabus and one exercise involved making a wrapper, in aluminium, to wrap round a pipe and be riveted into place.

One day, we were given two pieces of rough metal, a piece of cast iron about three inches square and one-and-a-half thick with a hole through the middle about three-quarters of an inch square. The other piece was a rough cube of brass with sides a little over one inch. Our task was to file the brass cube to exactly one inch per side, then file, or otherwise process the cast iron block until it was exactly three inches square by one inch thick and with a hole through its centre into which the brass cube would fit. The measurement tolerances on this job were quite frightening. An error of only one thousandth of an inch would allow a beam of light through the centre and incur penalties in the assessment. Halton apprentices have been making this test piece for many years until it has become recognised as representative of Halton engineering. It has been said, many times, that the old Halton Apprenticeship was the finest engineering training in the world.

Outside Kermode Hall, the building which housed the Schools, where we learned maths, physics, technical drawing, aerodynamics, etc., stands The Tribute, a permanent representation of the workpiece, many times lifesize, which was unveiled by Her Majesty Queen Elizabeth II in October 1997 to commemorate No.1 School of Technical Training at RAF Halton from 1922 to 1993.

In the Church at Halton there is another piece of work which, in a way, commemorates the man who was responsible for my basic training, Harry Tatem. Harry made the Lectern that supports the Bible. It is a model, in brass sheet, of a World War 1 biplane. Beautifully made and thoroughly polished, it is a lasting tribute to a real gentleman.

Our group was being trained as Engine Fitters, which included all the different parts and services needed to run the engine efficiently. Carburettors govern the flow of fuel into the engine through all sorts of conditions from sea level to, perhaps, thirty thousand feet in altitude, delivering full power for take-off and climbing to economical cruising for a long flight to the target. Airscrews, whose blade angle could be altered to facilitate economy, were also the responsibility of the engine fitter. Different types and makes of engines complicated the matter even further, involving different ignition systems, control systems, fuel pumps and tanks. Each of these topics would be taught by a specialist, who might be a member of the RAF or a civilian instructor. In all, the course was varied, complicated and, above all, very interesting. After taking notes all day, we would go back to our quarters after the evening meal and attempt to write up our notes, suitably embellished with intricate diagrams. We spent many hours copying charts and diagrams from various publications to make our notebooks as interesting and colourful as possible. Many of them were real works of art.

Throughout our two-year course, we could be assured of variety in our training. As well as our technical training, we were kept abreast of parade drills and carried out regular weapon training with rifles and hand grenades. Some of us found ourselves in the band playing drums, fifes or bagpipes. The Apprentices' Pipe Band, in particular, was in very strong demand to appear in local towns and villages on Saturdays throughout the summer, where fetes were being held to raise money to buy Spitfires. It was reckoned that every £5,000 raised would buy another Spitfire for the RAF, who desperately needed replacements for aircraft shot down. The bandsmen and their instruments would be taken in a bus to the required town where they would lead a parade through the streets. After the performance, the boys would be free to join the gathered crowds and, later, meet at a local venue for refreshments. Despite the resemblance to any other parade, these engagements were very popular with the band too. The boys were able to meet people who had nothing to do with the service, especially those delectable creatures called GIRLS, a commodity in very short supply at No.1 Wing, RAF Halton. Apart from the very few members of the Women's Royal Air Force who we might encounter in an office or at Sick Bay, we were actively discouraged from their society.

Wednesday and Saturday afternoons were our games afternoons; the rest of the week we were in workshops. Each month, three Sunday mornings were devoted to Church Parades. These were full-blown, grandiose affairs, which everybody must attend. All denominations were catered for in three churches and three separate parades. Most of us were Church of England and this was the largest parade; next came the Roman Catholics and finally the Other Denominations. In any such body of young men, probably women too, there will be a few who try to absent themselves from such occasions. Halton was not without its quota who would try almost anything to avoid Church Parades. In the majority of cases, they did not object to attending church, per se, the parade was the usual objection. One chap would regularly jump out of a top floor window onto a sloping bank below. His object was to sprain his ankle so that he was unfit for parade. Crazy? Of course, he must have been. I wonder if he enjoys his osteoarthritis now that he is old? On the remaining Sunday of the month, we were allowed a day pass which authorised us to leave camp up to a distance of 10 miles.

Once our duties for the day were completed, we were free to do as we wished, within limitations, until the time for lights out, 9.30pm. In inclement weather conditions we would probably head for the NAAFI canteen to play darts, snooker or any other game not involving money, or, perhaps if we were feeling rich, buy something to eat. If the weather was good, many of us, in twos and threes, would head for the hills. Halton Camp is situated in the shadow of the Chiltern Hills, which are covered in trees. We would roam for hours along narrow paths, sometimes visiting small villages and, occasionally, local hostelries. Very few Apprentices reached the age of eighteen years before the last six months of their course but local landlords did not seem to worry unduly about serving beer to under-age customers. Very occasionally, a lad would have a drop too much, a second half-pint perhaps, and his friends would have the onerous task of getting him back to his bed undetected.

Over and above all the expertise we learned from our studies, perhaps one of the most important things we learned was team spirit. No matter how complex a task there was always someone ready to help a poor struggler. We were communally responsible for the cleanliness of ourselves and our accommodation. Each occupant of a barrack room was allocated a particular task for the week, be it cleaning the Ablutions, the Toilets or any other part of the building, that area must be ready for inspection before we left for work. On rare occasions, a lad might be unwell or unready in some other way and there was always someone ready to give a hand with his "room job". This practice was important because, on active service, an aircraft must be ready on time no matter how busy the responsible tradesman might be. In the RAF, trade-barriers came down until the job was done; there were no trade unions to stop an engine fitter, for example, helping his airframe fitter colleague to change a wheel, or a master brake unit. They just got on with the job together.

The greater part of our course was spent working on component parts of the plane on a bench, but the final six weeks was spent on the airfield, on complete aircraft, learning Airfield Practice. Many varied topics came under the heading of airfield practice and we learned about knots and lashings, vital in heavy winds when aircraft could be overturned and damaged. We learned the importance of parking aircraft facing into the wind and which knots to use so the fastening would not slip.

Halton Apprentices receiving instruction.

Many of us had belonged to Boy Scouts, or similar organisations, but I doubt if any of us encountered so many different knots. Not only did we learn to tie the knots but also their correct usage. I had come across the Reef knot, Bowline and Slip knot, but things like the 'Bowline on a Bight' were completely new to me, as were Sheepshank, Manrope and Splicing.

Other important topics were marshalling signals for directing an aircraft to, or from, its parking place, fire drills and precautions and, the inevitable, paperwork. Any servicing carried out on an aircraft must be properly recorded in the appropriate Record Book (Form 700) and cleared by the Non-commissioned Officer in charge.

After the Airfield Phase we knew that Passing Out was looming into sight. Apart from very stringent testing we had to prepare for the Passing Out Parade. We had practised this ceremonial several times during our training, but now rehearsals were even more frequent and severe. On the day, the march past would be witnessed by a very senior officer who would also inspect every man on parade. In command of the troops would be the Senior NCO Apprentice whose future progress in the service could well be decided on his performance that day. Inevitably, there would be one or two boys on parade for whom the tension would prove to be too great. They would collapse and have to be carried off by medical orderlies strategically positioned around the square. With the parade over our time at Halton was almost finished.

Our final leave from Halton, Christmas 1943, was a fairly memorable experience for me. We were, of course, still in the middle of a war and food and fuel, etc., was strictly rationed. It was all the more surprising then, to find people holding Christmas parties. My parents would have willingly tried to give their support to such a venture but our little house was crowded with its normal five occupants. Fortunately, Don Small's parents and another friend's parents had much larger houses and both had planned to hold parties, to which I was invited.

The author at Halton.

At Don's house there were about eight of us and a good time was had by all. The meal over, to which most of us had contributed, the games began. Some of the guests were pairs of friends but there were enough singles for the remainder of us to pair off. We played the usual party games for that period, Blind Man's Buff, Pass the Parcel and Musical Chairs. Nothing very daring but we were all quite happy about that. I suppose the party broke up at about ten-thirty and we made our way home in the blackout.

The second party, a few days later, was a little different. It was held at the home of Jim, a good friend of Don and myself. Jim had a sister about three years older than us and she brought one of her school friends. I had met the sister before but the girl-friend was quite new to me. As I walked into the room where most of the guests were already, I saw this creature across the room. It sounds pretty corny to say so, but I think it was love at first sight for both of us. It seemed we could not take our eyes off each other and, once introduced, we had eyes for nobody else and spent almost all of the evening together. Molly, for that was her name, was about five feet seven inches tall with dark brown hair, brown eyes and the kind of figure men dream about. She was gorgeous! After the party we saw each other several times before I had to go back to Halton, but not before we had decided we wanted the relationship to continue.

Back at Halton, with a new interest in life, I found myself writing letters every few days; not previously a normal item on my agenda. The day before I left Halton I received, probably, the shock of my life. Exercising the lady's privilege, Molly proposed marriage to me on St Valentine's Day. It took me very much by surprise and, for a moment, I wondered if it could be a joke. Hoping that it was, in fact, a serious offer, I accepted immediately. The very next day I was posted to RAF Kirton-in-Lindsey, which, I learned, was just south of Scunthorpe in north Lincolnshire. I could not get home to see Molly for a few weeks but then we went to Sheffield and bought the ring.

Our relationship progressed and talk soon turned to the subject of matrimony. Molly, I learned, was about four years older than me and, at the age of 22, was keen to be married. But my pay, at that time, was about £1 17s 6d (£1.87) per week and although Molly had a good job and commensurate salary, life together would have been frugal, to say the least. We talked and planned, as young lovers will, but there seemed little chance of fulfilling our dreams at that time.

The War had been going on for more than four years and there was much speculation about the possibility of opening a Second Front – that is to say, an impending invasion of France.

I managed to get home, usually, on alternate Friday evenings for a weekend pass, when Molly would be waiting for me in the Gallery of the City Hall. She would buy two tickets, for the same pair of seats each time, for the Halle Orchestra Concert, and leave mine in the Box Office, in case I was late. After the concert we would go to her home and do our courting in the warmth of their sitting room. I rarely saw her parents, as they seemed to go to bed very early. We would listen to records, talk about our future and, generally, get to know each other. It was a happy time for us both.

8. Man's Service

I had been sent to Kirton-in-Lindsey along with about four or five other engine fitters and found it to be a medium-sized grass airfield where qualified pilots were being re-educated to fly Spitfires after being experienced on other aircraft such as Hurricanes, Defiants, etc. I was detailed to work under Corporal Skeggs, a conscript serving the duration of the war. I have no doubt he was a very competent tradesman but he hated ex-Apprentices or 'ex-brats', as he contemptuously called us. Many regular airmen, as well as conscripts, did not like us, as they feared we would be preferred for promotion. We were known as "Trenchard's Brats", since the apprentice scheme had been inaugurated by Air Chief Marshal Lord Trenchard in the early 1920's although some, not so kindly, referred to us as "Trenchard's Little Bastards" – but we won't go into that!

Soon after I joined his team, Corporal Skeggs was given the job of changing one cylinder block of a Rolls Royce Merlin engine *in situ* in a Spitfire. The Merlin engine had two blocks of six cylinders each, set at an angle of sixty degrees on a crankcase. To change the whole engine was fairly straightforward but to change one block was most unusual. Skeggsy set to work in his usual bad-tempered way and the job was completed in good time.

Meanwhile, the trainee pilots were causing us a lot of work. Apparently, in the Hurricane cockpit (with which the trainees were familiar), when on landing approach, in order to select 'Undercarriage Down' the pilot would move the control lever across its quadrant and the wheels would be lowered and locked. In the Spitfire a similar lever was moved but at the end of its travel it must be clicked into a 'gate' or it may revert to its former position due to vibration, with the result that the wheels would lower and then start to retract again. This could lead to the aircraft landing with no wheels in position.

In the month of March 1944, no less than 18 Spitfires landed with their wheels wholly or partly retracted at Kirton-in-Lindsey. Each time this occurred, the engine and propeller would have to be removed and thoroughly overhauled to eliminate any damage and, of course, there would be a repair programme for the underside of the plane. Fortunately, I cannot remember any cases of serious pilot damage.

9. Destination Unknown

I was at Kirton for only about three and a half months. On 6th June 1944 the Allied Forces invaded France and, on the same day, I and many of the apprentices who went there with me, were notified of our impending service overseas. Immediately we had to down tools, report to the Orderly Room and then visit almost all sections of the camp for 'clearance', to check that we had no outstanding loans, etc. By mid-afternoon we were on our way home for two weeks of Embarkation Leave to say goodbye to our families, etc. We all thought we were *en route* for Europe.

We met up again two weeks later at Blackpool, which was being used as a Transit Camp for overseas postings. Here we were given injections and inoculations against almost all diseases known and unknown. Film shows and lectures were arranged to warn us of the dangers of unprotected sex, the avoidance of Venereal Disease being the object rather than unwanted pregnancy.

After about two weeks of glorious sunny weather, we were told that we were to move on, with our kitbags stuffed with all kinds of new clothing. In order to prevent our guessing where we were bound, we had been issued with thick woollen under-wear as well as tropical khaki uniforms. We loaded into lorries for the journey to Liverpool. We arrived on the quayside in mid-afternoon where we lined up for inspection by His Majesty's Customs and Excise Department. I don't know what they expected to find, perhaps secret radio transmitters or even stowaways. All clear, we lined up again to climb the gangway of the SS *Moultan*, a converted merchantman of, I believe, some 16,000 tons. The ship had been fitted out to carry troops and there were about 6,000 of us coming aboard. The holds had been lined and fitted out as mess-decks with fixed tables and bench seats either side and, over the central area, hooks had been installed from which we hung hammocks for sleeping. Most of our kit had been consigned to the holds as 'Not Wanted On Voyage'. We were allowed to keep our washing and shaving kit and one change of clothing, after all, we had no idea where we were going or how long it would take.

We had embarked on the *Moultan* in late afternoon and had no sooner settled into our mess decks when the engines were started and we were on our way. Out across Liverpool Bay with the Liver Birds silhouetted against the evening sky, the ship drifted slowly and turned north through St George's Channel. The northerly course was maintained through the night and, in the morning light, we saw the docks of Gourock and the Clyde. After a brief stoppage we were under way again, still on our northerly course. Although we did not see them, we were told that we were part of a convoy.

The Captain of the *Moultan* spoke to us over the public address system and we learned that we were aboard the most heavily armed ship in this particular convoy. Our ship was armed with, amongst many smaller weapons, a six-inch gun on the after deck. In the event of an encounter with the enemy, we were duty bound to go into action and stay in action until the action ceased. Needless to say, we were not particularly pleased with our prospects but, there being very little we could do about it, we would just have to pray that there would be no action on this voyage.

Our northerly course showed little sign of a change and, although it was July, it began to feel cooler. After about thirty-six hours, the budding navigators amongst us noted a change of direction towards the west. This, of course, led to more speculation about our eventual destination. Two days later and we started to travel southwards and, after a while, there was speculation as to who would be the first to see the Statue of Liberty. In the complete absence of any information, rumours were rife. No-one was giving us any clues to build on, so rumours flew freely. The search for Liberty's torch ceased when we eventually turned towards the east. Now, it seemed, we were going back home to England. Some hopes!

During the sixth night of our journey, the ship lurched over and began to travel in a large circle, which was continued all through the night. There was no official announcement but, according to a friendly crewmember, a submarine had been detected close to the convoy and it had been decided to take evasive action. It later transpired that we had been about to enter the Straits of Gibraltar. This would involve the lowering of a great barrier stretched across the strait in order to prevent the entry of enemy ships into the Mediterranean Sea. The enemy submarine had, apparently, been trying to infiltrate itself into our convoy so as to gain access to the shipping in the Mediterranean. The convoy's circling manoeuvre appeared to have been successful so our previous course was resumed and, later, we had the pleasure of seeing the great Rock of Gibraltar on our left and the coastline of Morocco on our right. It was good to see dry land once more, the first since we left England more than a week ago.

There was no chance of a stop at Gibraltar and we sailed on quite close to the coast of North Africa. I suppose we must have been some three miles offshore but the weather was fine and sunny and almost everyone crowded the starboard rail to see as much as possible of the land. We learned, afterwards, that ours had been one of the first convoys to pass through the Mediterranean following the North African Campaign. Wherever we were to finish this journey, we were spared the tedious trip right round Cape Horn and a possible stay of a few days or weeks in South Africa. It would have been hard to endure such hardships, especially with the knowledge that we would have to get aboard the troopship once more to continue our journey.

The trip through the Mediterranean was uneventful and hot, until, that is, the last night when our beauty sleep was interrupted by sounds of heavy gunfire somewhere off to the north. By guesswork, we thought this might have been on the island of Crete, or possibly, Cyprus. However, it did not involve us and, the next morning, we slowed our pace and began to come closer to land. Suddenly we were called to boat stations there was a mad dash to get to our places. Miraculously, it seemed, the ship began to swing round to the right and resumed an even keel. Only then did we realise that, for several days, we had been sailing with a severe list to starboard. The captain had ordered us to boat stations in order to level the ship so that he could more easily negotiate the very narrow passageway through the entrance to the Suez Canal.

The docks of Port Said were almost blocked by damaged shipping awaiting repair or salvage. There were many ships, tied up to each other, with gaping holes through their hulls from one side to the other. Some had serious damage to their superstructure and most showed severe signs of burning. I think we all realised then how lucky we were to have had an action-free trip.

We wasted little time at Port Said and soon progressed towards the Suez Canal. Presumably, passages through the canal were regulated to one direction only at certain times of day. The canal is about ninety miles long but roughly mid-way there are the Bitter Lakes, where shipping in opposite directions can easily pass each other. On the west side of the canal, a road runs parallel, so we could see people and vehicles, not to mention camels and dogs. Progress was fairly slow and, I suppose, we took several hours to reach the lakes.

Here we stopped for a while and, in no time at all, there were flocks of small boats alongside with merchants offering for sale all kinds of fruits, nuts, mainly coconuts, small carvings of camels and boats, as well as watches and costume jewellery. Of course, the watches and jewellery were offered as the very best, expensive items, but I doubt if they would stand close examination. To carry out this business the merchants passed up small baskets attached to thin ropes.

After much haggling over the price of an item, the customer would send down the money and the merchant would send up the goods. On occasions, a wily customer would persuade the merchant to pass up the goods for inspection on the promise of cash by return. Predictably, there were one or two fraudulent attempts on both sides.

The progress of this al fresco market was interesting to watch as also the activities of small Arab boys who would dive to retrieve coins dropped from the ship's rail by passengers. Some of these boys were extremely competent swimmers and fully deserved any coins they managed to retrieve.

After a stop of an hour, or so, we were under way once more. By now we were fairly convinced that our destination was not to be Europe, but that still left a lot of very dangerous destinations, and there was still no indication of where it would be. Continuing our southerly journey we passed the memorial to Ferdinand de Lesseps, the French engineer responsible for the construction of this magnificent canal, and, after several hours more, we were out of the narrow waterway and into the open water of Port Suez. Once in clear water, the ship dropped anchor and we began to take stock of our new surroundings. There was quite a lot of shipping to be seen and this restricted our view of the port, to some extent. We stopped there for two days in very warm weather, and many of us wondered why we could not be allowed to have a swim, as the water looked very clear and clean and not too deep. The reason we were confined to the ship became very clear as the first evening drew in. Looking over the rail, we saw some small sharks circling the ship. I suppose they were only four or five feet in length but I have no doubt they had quite large teeth and voracious appetites. I did not mind waiting a few more days for my swim.

We stopped at Suez for about forty-eight hours and then, anchors aweigh, we were travelling south, once more, down the Red Sea. Our next stop was to be Aden, where several passengers disembarked. Some of these were Army personnel and the rest were RAF, no doubt on their way to the barren air force base at Khormaksar. After dropping off our colleagues and refuelling the ship, we were on the sea again sailing past the Horn of Africa and into the Arabian Sea.

We saw little of the coast as we sailed between the Yemen and Somalia, possibly as a security precaution, as these were, I believe, neutral countries. It now seemed certain that we would be paying at least a visit to India and this was confirmed when, about five weeks after leaving Liverpool, we turned towards Bombay.

The weather was extremely hot, the sun was a ball of fire and we were loaded up with all our kit as we made our way down the gangway on to the dockside. To the uninitiated, like me, one dock looks very like another. The main difference, I noticed at Bombay, was that there were lots of people, men presumably, scurrying about the dockside wearing white-ish clothing, rather like bed-sheets wrapped around their waists and between their legs. They looked very strange to me, as I had never seen anyone wearing a *dhoti* before. Later I was to learn that these people were known as 'coolies' and were the workhorses of India.

10. India – Jewel of the East

In groups, we were marched down the gangway and into waiting lorries which would take us to the Transit Camp a few miles outside Bombay, where we would spend the next few weeks whilst our postings were arranged. The Transit Camp was called Worli and consisted of wooden huts rather like the ones we have all seen in television series such as *Tenko* or anything portraying prison camps in the Far East jungles. Built on stilts about four feet above the ground, they had a central passageway, about four feet wide, with raised platforms on either side, on which our beds would be placed. Each hut was topped with a wooden roof and housed, perhaps, twenty-four men. The sides of the huts were open to allow free circulation of air and, therefore, kept reasonably cool. Mosquito nets were draped over each bed-space and tucked in under the edge of the "mattress" – a flat-pack of horsehair covered in rough canvas, not very comfortable but better than nothing.

Whilst in this transit camp we were required to attend talks, lectures and film-shows informing us of the dangers that might be encountered in India. Many areas were actively opposed to the presence of British troops in their country. So, we were told, "If you are driving a vehicle through these hostile areas, keep your speed up and do not stop for anything, including accidents". Talks also covered the subject of sex. These talks, in Bombay, were accompanied by films, made in America, showing, in extremely explicit detail, the results of venereal infection. They were enough to turn anyone against sex, protected or not, legal or not, for the rest of their normal life. The only advantage of being in the camp was its proximity to Bombay. We had quite a lot of free time and were able to make frequent visits to the city.

The camp was situated on raised ground beside a main road, on the other side of which there was a shanty town. Imagine a large area completely covered by small huts built from corrugated iron sheets, flattened petrol cans and occasional pieces of wood. These huts were really ramshackle and there were no toilet facilities. Standpipes had been placed at intervals so there was running water, but these had to be shared by families and strangers. Covered drains were not provided, instead shallow gullies drained away any surface water. We were told that approximately one million people lived in that town. After that piece of information, there were no more complaints about our accommodation.

Our trips to Bombay took us along clean made-up roads serving multi-story blocks of apartments surrounded by lawns and gardens tended by native workmen. One could judge, from the quality of curtains and the clothing worn by some of the occupants, that these were luxury apartments inhabited by fairly well-to-do people. Yet, within walking distance, a million people were surviving, but only just, in the utter squalor of that shanty town. This was my first and lasting impression of India, the enormous contrast between rich and poor. It was an all-pervading fact, on any railway station, from mid-afternoon, at least half of the width of the platforms would be covered by people lying on blankets, claiming their places for the coming night, whilst, around the corner of the street, there was a cinema, air-conditioned by day, but as night fell, the roof could slide open to keep the customers cool. I asked a young Anglo-

Indian boy what all these people do for a living. He shrugged his shoulders and said, "They beg, Sahib." Apparently, at that time, almost fifty per cent of the population lived by begging from the other half. To be fair, I must stress that this was wartime, when people tend to migrate to the cities, where there was, probably, a housing shortage anyway. Quite recently (2005) I met an Indian doctor in England, a native of Bombay, who assured me that the shanty town and, indeed, Worli had been demolished and was now an area of luxury apartments. I cannot say there are no longer poor people in India but I was pleased to hear that conditions in that area had been improved.

Since leaving home, at the end of my Embarkation Leave, I had not been able to write to my parents, or indeed to my fiancée, and it would be some time before I could possibly hear from them.

One day, we were called on parade and told to pack all our kit and be ready to move out the next morning. At last, something was to happen, we were not forgotten after all. The next day, Tuesday, which must have been close to the end of August, we were loaded onto the lorries again and driven to Bombay Railway Station, where we clambered on to a train. Although our trips from Worli had taken us on the local electric trains, we were not really prepared for the journey now starting. Train journeys in India tend to be measured in days rather than hours. The scenery, inevitably, is very varied and often quite spectacular.

Our trip started in Bombay at three o'clock on a Tuesday afternoon. The sunny weather we had enjoyed almost continuously since leaving home was starting to break up. They told us the monsoon was starting. Fortunately, the rain did not fall whilst we were loading ourselves on to the train. Once our kit was on board, many of us were occupied in haggling for fruit and cigarettes from the merchants who crowded the platforms.

When the monsoon starts the only place to be is indoors. No-one wilfully allows himself to be caught out in the storm. Nothing, I repeat nothing, in the way of clothing will stop the force of the rain. One moment the sky is reasonably clear, then, as if from nowhere, a cloud looms up and, lo, we have a monsoon. After, perhaps, only fifteen minutes, the sky is clear again and the hot sun does everything it can to bring one to the boil as quickly as possible. On other occasions the rainfall may last several hours and local flooding is commonplace.

Our train eventually started to move and our second journey into the unknown began. This train was electrically powered and, after travelling about thirty miles through the suburbs of Bombay, we sensed it begin to climb. The upward passage seemed as if it would never end. Next came a series of tunnels numbering about ten in a space of, perhaps, another thirty miles. Seeing those tunnels, hewn through solid rock, one could only wonder at the technology and skill that had made it possible. Apart from the absence of bridges, this journey was similar to one through Cornwall, all twists and turns through hills of all sizes. Sometime during this day, our electric engine was replaced by a steam locomotive.

As is usual in India, nightfall came early and, after playing cards for a while, we thought it wise to turn in. Our beds were the seats we had been sitting on all day; wooden bunks with seat cushions of leather, stuffed with horse-hair, each about six feet long and two feet wide. I slept not at all badly. Blankets were unnecessary, which saved a lot of space.

I was awakened by the sound of Indian voices and realised that the train was stationary at a platform. I clambered down from my upper bunk and busied myself with washing, shaving and generally making myself ready for breakfast. Most of our food on board was cold, though we were provided with one hot meal per day. There was always hot water from the engine and someone had thoughtfully included containers to collect it.

Before the train moved on, I noticed a young boy on the platform who looked very English. I beckoned him over and had a pleasant conversation with him. He spoke good English, though with a strong American accent. His parents, apparently, were English and had come to live in India about sixteen years previously. He had never seen England, being only fourteen years of age, but his ambitions included a visit to our homeland. The boy said he thought India was alright, except for the climate. He should do well in England; most people think there is not much wrong with it apart from the climate.

On Wednesday, the second day of our journey, the countryside through which we were passing looked very similar to an English one, except for the occasional clusters of banana trees. We passed over many river gorges during this journey, some were very deep but in others we could see herds of water buffalo basking in the shallow water. In some areas, close to the track, we could see waterlogged fields reminiscent of rice fields. It seemed that the families who tended these crops often lived in little hovels by the edge of their fields, some of them little more than a thatch roof supported by half a dozen poles. The scenery here was composed of grassland with occasional clumps of shrubs here and there as far as the eye could see.

The conditions on the train were much better than we had expected. After the terribly crowded conditions on the ship and the awful tales we had heard about Indian transport, with as many people on the outside of the train as there were inside, we expected much worse discomforts. At one of our stops, a Station Master told us we had about three hundred miles to go and this would mean thirty-six to forty-eight hours more travelling. The apparent slowness of our progress was explained by the fact that we were on a "special" train that made frequent stops and was, at fairly frequent intervals, shunted into a siding to allow the passage of more important trains. This was necessary because much of the track we were on was single track.

On Thursday, it was very hot indeed and most of the lads removed their shirts. The landscape looked very green, broken here and there by a wide river gorge, often with no water in it. The land was very flat indeed, which probably accounted for the extreme width of the river beds. In the far distance we saw a long, low range of hills. Some of the peaks seemed to have their heads in a low cloud belt, which seemed to indicate the possibility of rain. That night we reached our destination, Cawnpore, in Uttar Pradesh as it was then called. Since the partition of India and Pakistan, the city has changed its name to Kanpur.

Our journey had taken fifty-seven hours from 3pm Tuesday until midnight on Thursday. An indication of Indian Rail Transport is given in this extract from an order issued on that Thursday. *"We are due to arrive at our destination sometime between 1900hours and 23.59 hours tonight".* We actually arrived at 23.50 hours so we were within our schedule.

After a short wait on the station we were divided into parties according to our final destinations and taken to waiting lorries which took us to our various units in the area where we were extremely pleased to have a good meal followed by a good night's sleep.

11. Cawnpore

Our first impressions of Cawnpore were very unfavourable. When one visits India one meets a thousand-and-one new smells. On reaching Cawnpore one finds another.

On arrival at Cawnpore I was told I had been posted to TP1, which did not mean very much to me. With twenty other men I was delivered to a camp and, after a meal, went to bed and slept like a baby. The next morning we learned that TP1 was an acronym for Technical Project No 1. It was, to all intents and purposes, a huge factory with a large number of bays devoted to the complete overhaul of aircraft engines and cockpit instruments. We later learned that these components belonged to aircraft which had landed at an airfield some fourteen miles away after being flown from forward bases in Burma. Each of the two parts of this set-up had around five thousand men, making the overall unit one of the largest in the RAF. We were to be members of No.322 Maintenance Unit.

After the usual arrival procedure, during which we were allocated to various sections, I, along with three or four of my friends, was told that we would be working the night shift so we had the rest of that day to prepare ourselves for work commencing at five pm. None of us had any experience of night work, or indeed of factory work for that matter. At about four o'clock we gathered at the lorry park where we met the rest of the night workers, who numbered quite a few. There was a certain amount of banter but on the whole we were made to feel reasonably welcome. Like most newcomers to an existing system, we were, of course, allocated the mind-bendingly boring jobs. I was to work on cleaning and degreasing engine parts using toxic materials. Whilst smoking was permitted in most parts of the factory, I was strictly forbidden any smoking materials. I was told that the fumes from my cleaning bath, if breathed through a cigarette, would produce something similar to Phosgene, a life-threatening poison. It was a boring job and the fumes were rather unpleasant but I did the best I could. As luck would have it, I did not keep the job for more than a couple of weeks.

It appeared that Cawnpore had a small Civil Airport on the edge of town, which had been taken over by the RAF and was in use as a Research and Development Unit. This was a small unit of perhaps 150 men, who carried out investigations into problems which arose from operating aircraft designed for temperate climates in sub-tropical conditions. The Engineering Officer from this unit had come to TP1 and selected a few people from the newcomers. I have no idea what criteria were used for this selection, unless it was that the selectees were ex-Halton apprentices. Whatever the reason, yours truly was on his way to the Civil Airport.

The airport was quite small, having only one runway about 900 yards long, an Administration Building and, at the other end of the runway, a Workshop Building and a small hangar. The officers were housed at Chakheri, the main airfield for 322 M.U., about three miles from R&D Unit. The other ranks were housed in one of the blocks, known as Wheeler's Barracks (about which more later) adjacent to the Civil Airport and only about one mile from the city.

Wheeler's Barracks were built in the 1850s to accommodate about one thousand men of the Army. They consisted of seven stone buildings, each about 200 feet long, 60 feet wide and roughly 50 feet high. They were built in very troubled times for the Raj and the walls were some three feet thick. The blocks were laid out in echelon formation with, near one end of the row, a cookhouse and dining room. Opposite each block was a washhouse with sinks, of stone, and shower cubicles which could, if necessary, accommodate six or eight men at a time. There was no heating in the barracks and no hot water for washing but for most of the year such things would be a luxury. Nevertheless, I can remember several times, in winter, when it would have been very nice to feel a warm spray. In spite of the lack of heating and hot water, life in the barracks was fairly comfortable.

Being isolated from the main units meant that we were quite free to walk into the city, at least to that part which was not Out of Bounds for servicemen. It was estimated that the population of Cawnpore was around five million at the commencement of World War II but only one street, the Mall, was in bounds. When the war started the population increased as people flocked in to find work. The Mall was very popular with a wide variety of shops, cafés and restaurants and even a cinema showing English speaking films, fairly up-to-date ones too.

Cawnpore had been at the centre of the Indian Mutiny in 1857 and has a terrible history of that period. There were various monuments in the city, including the site where the British families had been housed. The mutineers attacked this area and the British defended it stubbornly. After a period of stand-off, the rebel leader offered the British their freedom and this was accepted in good faith but, as the troops moved out from their cover, the rebels opened up with machine-gun fire and killed most of the soldiers. The remainder of the British, mainly women and children, were driven to a deep well where they were shot and all – dead and survivors – thrown into the well. When peaceful conditions were restored, the well was sealed with a marble statue of an angel and surrounded by a decorative wall. This was designed by an Italian sculptor, commissioned personally by Their Majesties Queen Victoria and her husband Albert. Following Partition in 1947, these memorabilia have been removed and re-erected in the Garrison Graveyard.

For most of the time that I spent in Wheeler's Barracks the remaining blocks were unoccupied. By some means, of which I am not certain, we had access to the ground floor of a block which had been fitted out as a gymnasium. At that time I was very keen to keep myself in good shape so I was happy to use the facilities provided. Each morning, before breakfast and before any of my colleagues were awake, I would jog along to the gym and work out with exercises and punch-bags for 30 or 40 minutes. I have never been fanatical about physical fitness but I always enjoyed the discipline of boxing training.

R&D Unit was engaged in a number of trial installations and investigations. Many of our investigations were of faults in performance, of various aircraft, due, in whole or in part, to the atmospheric conditions. As I mentioned previously, most of our aircraft had been designed with a European climate in mind. In the late thirties and early forties few people would have expected us to be fighting in the Far East. Even allowing for the vagaries of climatic variations in Europe, we could have been forgiven for not expecting one hundred per cent humidity of the monsoon or the 100+ degrees of an average Far Eastern summer. This caused all kinds of aberrations in the performance of aircraft; vapour locks could occur in fuel line causing engines to fail, for example. All these had to be investigated in a wide variety of aircraft. Our dispersal area might hold, at any one time, all or a selection of the following: Halifax bomber, Beaufighter, Spitfire, Liberator, Mustang, Hurricane, Tempest, we even had a Tiger Moth, a Harvard Trainer and an Auster Army Observation aircraft.

Apart from the investigations into the performance, or otherwise, of front line aircraft, we did a great deal of work on other aspects of the war. In Burma the weather was so hot and humid that servicing crews were being held back from their jobs because aircraft were, quite literally, too hot to handle. The metal skin of the aircraft would be untouchable and, inside the craft, men were fainting because of the heat. We were given the job of designing and building air blowers. The Unit Engineering Officer designed a machine which could be brought close to an aircraft and, via a duct, could blow cool air into the cockpit. The concept of this machine was fairly simple. A metal tray some six inches deep and about two feet square was filled with water and a drum, double-walled and with the intervening space filled with hay, was made to rotate on a horizontal spindle mounted above the tray. As the drum rotated, the hay was kept wet and air, blown through the hay, was cooled and could be ducted into the aircraft body. Many different variations of this design were built, modified and rebuilt until, eventually, a model was submitted to a local factory for multiple production.

Another task we performed concerned the thick jungle foliage which obscured the view of ground attack aircraft and hid enemy forces. This problem became so urgent that the higher command decided the time had come for defoliation on a large scale. Wide stretches of jungle were to be sprayed from the air with powerful chemical defoliants. R&D's job was to fit large tanks inside the fuselages of Dakotas and Liberators to hold the chemicals and the pipe-work necessary to spray the jungle.

Whilst the idea may have been good, even successful, the ecological and human destruction caused a great deal of criticism and protest.

R&D may have been a small unit but we had number of enthusiastic footballers. We managed to field two teams which played in the league tournaments of Chakheri, the nearer part of the maintenance unit. Twice each week, after the day's work was done, two 3-ton lorries would leave the Civil Airport filled with players and spectators. Both our teams did well in the league tables. Towards the end of the 1944-45 season our No 1 goalkeeper was stricken with Typhus and, for some weeks, was confined to a hospital bed fighting for his life. Although he made something of a recovery, he never played football for us again and was shipped back home to the UK as soon as he was fit to travel.

At about this time, early 1945, it was decided that our work would be carried out much more efficiently if the workshop could be made cooler. So, it was decided that we should build an underground workshop. The first stage was to dig a pit, near the edge of the airfield, some fifty feet long, twenty-five feet wide and seven feet deep, the idea being to construct a building in the pit and then cover it with the spoil we had dug out. Every man who could be spared took part in the digging whenever he could be there. Digging commenced early in the year and, long before it was finished, the heat was becoming unbearable.

One morning I woke up to find my left hand swollen like a boxing glove and very painful. Of course, being in a sub-tropical country, I took myself off to see the Medical Officer. This involved a walk across rough country for nearly half-a-mile to the Army Hospital. As we were so far from the other two RAF stations our needs were supplied by this hospital. On sight of my hand, the MO sent for someone to see me into the nearest bed. I was inspected by the Senior Surgical Officer, appropriately named Captain Sawyer, who said he would open up my hand, insert a drain under the muscle controlling my little finger, and drain out the fluid causing the distortion of my hand. All went well, except that someone made the mistake of taking me into the operating theatre the wrong way round. The surgeon was rather upset and made them take me out and bring me in the right way.

When I came round from the anaesthetic, back in the ward, a pretty young nurse came to see me with a miniature cake on a saucer and a candle on top. She had been reading my documents and had realised that day was my birthday. I was just 19 years old. She could not have been much older herself and it was a very nice gesture. I stayed in the hospital for about ten days and, as I was being discharged, Capt. Sawyer looked at my hand critically. One side of the wound stood above the other and he said, "That should be alright. If it doesn't smooth out, come back and we'll have another go." I learned from other patients that this was his normal reaction and nothing for me to worry about.

Returning to my unit, I found the digging was still in progress but I was to be excused digging, at least for the time being. I never did find out, for certain, what had caused my injury in the first place. It was suggested that perhaps I had an injury, but there was no sign of any injury to my left hand.

I had a blister or two on my right hand but they appeared to be healing quite well. It was then suggested that the blisters were the cause of the trouble. Perhaps one had become infected and the poison had travelled round my body until it found a weakness, in my left hand, where it gathered. It sounded a bit far-fetched but it was the best explanation I could get.

By this time we were getting into May and the end of hostilities in Europe. Very soon most of the men of R&D Unit would be expecting to go home. Unfortunately, this process took rather longer than expected and tension built up. We heard that troops who had been serving in Europe were being demobilised and were getting back into civilian employment. But the war in the Far East was still very much on-going. As regular members of the RAF, I and many of my colleagues had no reason to complain. We had been posted to India to do a tour of duty and the normal tour in India was four years.

One morning, as we arrived for work, we were separated into two groups, Regulars and Conscripts. We regulars were addressed by the Commanding Officer, who told us that there had been a Call For Action by the conscripts. In short, they were being called out on strike. We were advised that, from our point of view, there was nothing to be gained by joining their action. In fact, it was probable that any demonstration of support on our part might have a very detrimental effect on our future careers. I think we all realised the wisdom of this warning and carried on with our work as far as possible.

As we at R&D, were not in constant touch with the large units, we were not kept informed of the actions being taken by the conscripts. However, over the next week or two news began to filter through. Large numbers of conscripts had put down their tools and stopped work. Meetings were held to hear their main complaints and discover what would be required to regain their cooperation. The main cause for complaint seemed to be the different rates at which conscripts were being demobilised in Europe and the Far East. A programme had been published showing the dates at which various groups of men would be returned to civilian life. Problems arose when it was discovered that men in Europe, classed in the same group as their colleagues in the India, were being released up to three months earlier, which meant that, in the post-war scramble for employment, they had a three month advantage. Our friends in India feared that there would be no jobs left when they finally got home. Much discussion took place and meetings were held in darkened hangars for fear of reprisals.

The delayed demobilisation was not the only cause for complaint. We, at the civil airport, were in primitive but fairly comfortable conditions whereas on some of the larger units conditions were much more unpleasant, so much so that at Chakheri the troops had, for some time, threatened to burn the place down as soon as the Far East War was over. Indeed, when that war was declared over, fires broke out at Chakheri and TP1 and a fair amount of damage was caused at both places.

Eventually the war was completely over and a steady stream of conscripts on their way home. Life for the remainder of us was much quieter but we still had plenty to do. One of our most urgent tasks was to move R&D Unit out of the civil airport and into one of the huge hangars at Chakheri. Everything must go except one aircraft, a Tempest, which was unserviceable and awaiting spares from the UK. When these arrived it would be made serviceable and flown to its new home.

We soon settled in to our new quarters which, in some ways, were much more convenient. We were, of course, much further from the bright lights of Cawnpore but Chakheri had a fair selection of shops and its own cinema cum concert hall. With our enormous hangar there was much less need to work outside in the scorching sun. We were, of course, a much smaller unit now, with, perhaps forty personnel, one Warrant Officer engineering officer, one pilot and the Commanding Officer who, also, was an engineer. Our aircraft, at this time, consisted of two Tempests, a Harvard trainer and an Auster Army co-operations aircraft. When work was slack, I often flew with the pilot in the Harvard or the Auster. We got on very well and, after a while, he would let me take over the controls. This was my first experience of controlling an aircraft and I enjoyed the experience.

Whilst I was serving in India I was fortunate in being able to go on leave in the foothills of the Himalayas on more than one occasion. My first trip was to an Army Leave Camp at a place called Chakrata, situated about fifty miles north-west of Dehra Dun on a hilltop overlooking the upper reaches of the River Ganges. The camp was organised and run by the British Army and provided accommodation for British servicemen and women on leave. On arrival we were booked in and given a questionnaire to find out our interests. The answers were collated and activities arranged to suit most peoples' tastes.

I was only there for a week and put down football as my main interest. Next morning I found myself on a list with ten other names and learned that we were to be known as Team 5. All such teams were randomly selected so one might find oneself in a team containing 11 would-be goalkeepers or centre forwards. The method used for selection was reckoned to be as fair as any other and seemed to work quite well. The tournament started that morning so there was to be no hanging about waiting for a game. My team blended quite well and we did well in the opening rounds. Surprise, surprise, we found ourselves in the final. I had always played in defence but, there being a surplus of defenders, I found myself playing on the left wing. The final game was fairly even and at half-time there was no score. I noticed that when the opposing goalkeeper kicked the ball from the right-hand corner of his area it landed, quite often, just left of the centre circle in our half of the field. In the second half I positioned myself accordingly and, sure enough, the ball came to me. All I had to do was to return the ball with the inside of my boot and it soared into the net before he could get back to it.

I was the hero of my team for all of ten seconds. Unfortunately, the other team scored twice in that second half so we had to be satisfied with runner-up medals. The pitch, incidentally, was, quite literally, on top of a mountain, the top of which had been bulldozed to make a flat area and surrounded by a chain-link fence to prevent balls being lost over the side. Although the fence was about fifteen feet high, during that week two or three balls were lost over the side.

My second leave was at another hill-station called Naini Tal (the 'Tal' being Hindi for 'Lake'), in the same region as Chakrata but further to the south-east and about sixty miles from Mohradabad. Nainital was one of the hill-stations to which officers' and civil-servants' wives were evacuated in the hot season to escape the terrible heat. It was probably one of the biggest and most popular hill-stations in the northern region of Uttar Pradesh province. It is still in operation and figures prominently in several Travel Agents' brochures today. I went there along with another corporal from R&D Unit in early December 1946.

On arrival we met up with two Navy men and formed a foursome, which kept us in company for our two-week stay. The village is built round the lake at an altitude of about 8,000 feet. Considering the altitude, the time of year and the region, the weather was remarkably pleasant. We could never decide whether the lake was the result of a man-made wall or a landslide. The water was extremely cold, so swimming was not really an option, but we often hired boats and rowed up and down the lake. Being young, fit and active, we did a fair amount of walking in the hills and discovered some spectacular waterfalls.

Admiring the view at Nainital.

Another pastime was riding. We could hire horses for very little cash, for an hour or for a day and go further up into the hills, which was very interesting. The lake is surrounded by mountains and on top of one of these we found a flattened area which had been paved and surrounded by a low stone wall. In the middle was a table with a carved notice, which identified it as "Dorothy's Seat". A nearby plaque explained that Dorothy had been the wife of a Government official and, following a serious illness, had come to Naini Tal to recuperate. Her bearer (servant) would have carried her to the top of the hill, where she would sit for several hours each day, reading and enjoying the beautiful views.

The horse riders.

Towards the end of our holiday, we decided to hire the horses for a whole day from early morning. With a pack of sandwiches for lunch, we would make a longer ride through the hills. We collected the horses and climbed aboard, setting off along the path which led to the hills. Passing the Cinema, on the outskirts of the village the horses began to trot. The track was unpaved and about fifteen feet wide, and, being early morning, there were few pedestrians about. As we came to a level piece of road, my horse broke into a gallop and my friends followed suit. My horse was in the lead as we approached a fork in the track.

Just at that moment, a young Indian boy ran across the road in front of me. A horse will never willingly run over someone and my mount veered to the right up a narrower track. Unfortunately, a line of coolies, carrying logs on their backs, was coming down the track and, of course, one of them got out of line. His largest log struck my right leg about half way between knee and ankle. The coolie went spinning, spraying the rest of his logs all around and my horse, no doubt sensing trouble, slowed to a standstill.

My friends caught up with me and helped me off the horse. There was blood everywhere. My trouser leg was torn, my shoe was full of blood and chaos reigned all around. Fortunately, the coolie was not injured. I was the only casualty and, with a large handkerchief wrapped around my leg, I was hoisted back on the horse and we turned to ride to the Army hospital about a mile through the village. I apologised to my friends for spoiling their day and they assured me that it was no problem. Once they had dumped me at the hospital, they would probably carry on with their ride anyway. Such sympathy can be most moving!

Our journey to the hospital took rather a long time because I was in pain and could not bear to be bounced about, my leg was very sore and we all thought it was probably broken. On reaching the hospital, the first notice we saw said, "NO HORSES

BEYOND THIS POINT," at which point we could barely see the entrance. My pals parked their mounts and escorted me, mounted, right up to the Main Entrance. I was accepted as a *bona fide* patient and helped down from the horse. My friends left to return to their mounts and I was helped into an empty ward and told to undress and get into bed.

It transpired that I was one of only two patients in the place. The other chap was fighting for his life against a bad dose of Malaria and must be kept in isolation, so they had to open another ward for Yours Truly. Examination showed that there was no broken bone but the wound was as deep as it could be on the front of my shin, so I had to stay in bed and have my leg bandaged until it healed. Apparently, such wounds are very slow to heal at altitude and it would be dangerous for me to travel back to my unit until it was better. I was in that hospital for about a week, living in the lap of luxury with a friendly doctor and several pretty nurses. What could be better? This was 1946 and perilously close to the end of my tour of duty in India. My greatest worry was that I might be stuck in the hospital when I should be clearing from R&D prior to travelling to Bombay to catch a boat. I explained this to the doctor, who was very sympathetic and let me out at the earliest possible moment, December 21st. I travelled back to Cawnpore in time to clear up all my business, pack up my kit and celebrate Christmas with my friends before catching the train on 27th December.

My train journey back to Cawnpore was not without incident. I had always found Indian train crews very friendly and helpful so, having stowed my kit in a compartment, I walked along to the engine for a chat. The driver was Anglo-Indian and spoke very good English. As the departure time got nearer he invited me to travel on the footplate for a while. It was early evening when we set off and would soon be dark. The metre gauge line from Mohradabad to Lucknow passes through jungle close to what is now the Corbett National Park.

Whilst on the footplate I gave a hand with stoking the boiler, the crew having demonstrated how the fuel must be evenly spread to avoid any hot-spots, which could damage the fire-box. They also drew my attention to points of interest outside the train.

On the front of the engine was a very powerful light, which illuminated the track for a long way in front of the train on straight parts of the line. Suddenly, the driver drew my attention to something crossing the line, perhaps two hundred yards in front of us. It was a full-grown tiger, who just ambled across the line as if he owned it. I have seen a good many wild animals on my travels but never, before or since, such a magnificent specimen. At the next stop I returned to my carriage for a sleep before we reached Lucknow, where we would transfer to a train with Standard gauge for the last forty or so miles to Cawnpore.

Back on camp, I was greeted by my friends who had been wondering if I would miss the boat. They should have known me better than that! I reported to the Commanding Officer of R&D Unit, who congratulated me on my recovery. I felt a bit of a fraud, really, because my leg, the cause of all the trouble, was not at all painful – it just would not heal. Everybody joked that a breath of sea air would probably work wonders and I had to agree. A quick dash round all the relevant sections and I was cleared and ready to start packing.

There was only one query regarding my clearance from the station. Some time ago I had found a load of bicycle parts and had built myself a bike. It was very useful because Chakheri was a large camp (currently the large Kanpur Airport) and riding was much quicker than walking. One evening I cycled to the camp cinema and, as usual, left the bike propped against the wall along with, perhaps, 200 other cycles. In fact, whilst I stood there, two other chaps came along and leaned their bikes on mine.

To cut a long story short, when I came to collect my bike it had disappeared although the two that had been on top of mine were still there and intact. I did not think too badly of it at the time but when it came to 'clearance', some two months later, my scrap bike was listed as issued to me and my inability to return it cost me £15 – not a large sum of money at today's prices but in 1946 that was two weeks' pay!

12. Homeward Bound

By this time it was December 23rd and everyone was packing up for Christmas holiday. Many of the lads had clubbed together for a Hut Party. Our hut was no exception and, I can assure you, we had a very good time that Christmas. Fortunately, I was able to sober up and put my kit, and, of course myself, on the ubiquitous lorry for the trip to Cawnpore railway station. The journey to Bombay seemed to take forever, but, I suppose, it was not much more than thirty-six hours which is not too bad for a journey of almost eight hundred miles. I do not remember too much about my second visit to Worli but no doubt most of my time was taken up with documentation. The troopship docked and we all piled on board. The vessel was the *Cameronian*, which was bigger, I believe, than the *Moultan* but with far fewer passengers. The war had been over for several months and, I suppose, fewer troops were in transit.

We left Bombay on 4th January 1947, when the temperature was 94 degrees Fahrenheit. The journey across the Arabian Sea passed without incident and we continued up the Red Sea and through the Suez Canal. Once more the small boats of the 'maritime market' were alongside whenever we came to a halt but, I feel, business was considerably slacker this time and bargains were harder to strike. On leaving Port Said we were told that we would divert to Piraeus, the port of Athens, Greece. This was not an enormous deviation from our course and was made in order to pick up the crew of a Greek ship which had been to Glasgow for repairs. Apparently, the ship had been commandeered during the war and was now being returned to its rightful owners.

Soon after we left Port Said, we ran into a storm. Sailors say that storms in the Mediterranean are "storms in a teacup". My only reply to that would be, "If that is the case then I have no wish to experience a storm in a bigger receptacle!" The wind was tremendous and the rain seemed as if it would never reach the sea; it was raining horizontally. Huge waves were breaking over the bows of the ship and, often, over the bridge. As usual, on troopships, the troops take turns to be Mess Steward and collect and serve their table. On that day it was my turn to do the honours. For lunch we had braised liver with mashed potatoes, green vegetables and onion gravy. Very few of the troops seemed to want to eat that day and those who did seemed to lose their food soon after.

Towards evening, the storm showed no sign of abating and, as if things were not bad enough already, we heard, on the BBC News, relayed through the public address system, that another Greek ship had struck a mine, probably broken loose by the storm, and had sunk with all hands. The ship had been on the way to Piraeus, on the same course as ourselves, about six hours ahead of us. The Captain altered course, in the hope of rescuing survivors but although searchlights had been erected on both sides of the ship, we saw nothing. The atmosphere on board was very taut, to say the least, and everyone was pleased to see land in the early morning.

We did not actually dock in the port but dropped anchor and waited for the Greek seamen to come out on a tender. Piraeus looked to be an interesting place with buildings along the seafront and a row of hills behind. The storm had almost abated when we resumed our course, once more, and, though the sea was still rough, it was much more pleasant than the day previous. There were, fortunately, no more incidents to report as we sailed westwards towards Gibraltar and then the Atlantic. We did have another, traditional, rough patch as we crossed the Bay of Biscay but it was not nearly as bad as our previous experience. A couple of days later we were close to our destination in bonny Scotland but our journey was not to end without another hold-up.

We docked in the Clyde on a Saturday morning towards the end of January. For the time of year the weather was mild and the sun threatened to shine but, as luck would have it, it was a big day in Scottish Football. The Scottish Football Cup tournament had brought together the 'old firm' – Glasgow Rangers were to meet Glasgow Celtic. The railways were busy, the streets were crowded and the Police were so stretched they decided we could not be allowed to disembark, so we had to stay on board and watch the tide rise and fall from 6.30 am till about 6 o'clock in the evening. It was galling but there was nothing we could do about it.

Eventually we were allowed to carry our kit down the gangway and onto a train, which took us to RAF Burtonwood in Lancashire, near Warrington. There, I must say, the Transit Centre staff were extremely efficient. In spite of it being a Saturday night, which could have been an excuse for anything, they gave us a meal, and fitted us all up with Travel Warrants, Ration books and Leave passes. We were then taken to railheads at Warrington and Manchester for trains to our home stations. I was pleased to climb aboard a train for Sheffield, although it was almost 10pm. Outside, heavy snow was falling, almost everywhere in England, they said. My train would take me through the Peak District and Chinley Tunnel before reaching

Sheffield. All went well and, the next day, we realised that my train had been the last to successfully pass through Chinley. The tunnel was closed for several days because of the snow. My parents were pleased to see their wandering boy, even if it was nearly two am.

The shock of the contrast between our departure from Bombay and my arrival in Sheffield was enormous. I suppose it must have been softened, to some extent, by the four-week sea trip but it was still a shock. The real softening of the blow came in the afternoon of that first day. Molly, my fiancée, came to my parents' house straight from her place of work and, then, my rehabilitation really began. Two-and-a-half years is a long time to be separated from the ones you love and leaves its mark on any relationship.

The weather certainly did not favour us as the snow, alternating with partial thaws and severe re-freezing caused havoc all over the United Kingdom. Each day the radio told us how bad the effects were in other parts of the country, but we needed no telling about the situation in Sheffield. Within a very few days there were shortages of all kinds of essentials. Many roads, including many of the busier, city centre roads, had a thick layer of ice which could not be moved even though the authorities had called in heavy earth-moving equipment. Bulldozers and graders, normally used to clear and landscape building sites, could not cope with the situation.

Gradually, the city was forced to a standstill. Shops were running short of foodstuffs because the wholesalers could not deliver. Sheffield, at that time, had seven breweries, but public houses were running short of beer. Under the terms of their licences, these pubs had to remain open, even if they had nothing to sell. Our milk was delivered, in normal times, by the farmer who produced it. Each morning, after milking his cows, he would load a two-wheeled cart with two ten-gallon urns of fresh milk and set off to deliver to his customers, some six miles away. All through that big freeze he came, wrapped up like an untidy parcel, perhaps a little later than usual.

As conditions got worse, he found it more and more difficult to complete his round and was faced with the prospect of throwing his hard-earned milk down a drain. One day, when he felt particularly low, he popped into the local pub to see if he could buy a drop of whisky to warm himself. Chatting with the landlord, discussing their mutual problems, they realised they could help each other. In spite of having no beer, the landlord had to stay open and entertain customers, who came in for a game of snooker or darts or dominoes, or perhaps just for a warm. If he could buy the farmer's surplus milk, perhaps he could sell it to his customers to lubricate their throats. It was worth a try, so a deal was made. It worked very well indeed. The farmer sold his surplus milk, the landlord had something to offer his clientele and the game-players could wet their whistles.

My Disembarkation Leave was, initially, for four weeks and the weather showed no signs of improving. Molly was working, as usual, five days per week, so I stayed at home, usually in bed to keep warm. Of course, the coal merchants had great problems with deliveries so house fires were small affairs. Housewives had to try to keep their fires alight to prevent the hot-water systems from freezing up. They soon learned the art of keeping the fire alight by covering the coals with the ash from yesterday's fire. This way, the heat was kept in the fireplace and heated the water in the back-boiler rather than the room.

Each day, I would rise about four in the afternoon, wash, shave and have a meal, then, about five-thirty, I would set out to go to Molly's home. Fortunately, Sheffield had a bus route which went round the city, linking the suburbs, called the 'circular route'. Both our homes were on the edge of town but about five miles apart. By taking this bus I could be at Molly's home about the time she arrived home from work.

Getting back to my home was a different problem, because, having so much time to make up, I'm afraid it was after midnight when I left her. By then the buses had stopped running so I had to walk home. At first I would retrace the route by which I had arrived but that was quite hilly and deserted at that time of night. I found that if I walked towards the centre of the city, I could almost always be offered a lift by patrolling policemen. They would take me to their headquarters and then I had only two-and-a half miles to walk. On rare occasions, I might get a lift from other policemen. I got to know some of these coppers very well and one night, when the snow was starting to fall, they offered me a cell for the night. I thanked them and quipped that they would have to catch me first!

13. Kirton-in-Lindsey Again

That winter was said to have been the worst in Britain since records began. When my disembarkation leave expired, I was told to report to Kirton Lindsey, my new posting.

Of course, I knew my life of luxury and idleness would inevitably come to an end sometime, but I hardly expected to be going back to the station I had left to go to India. I arrived there in the early evening, phoned for transport and booked in at the Guardroom. There were three of us arriving at the same time and a Warrant Officer, who was on duty, found us a nice warm Drying Room and a pile of blankets.

"Can't think why they have sent you here," he said. "The camp closed down at lunchtime. Everybody has gone home. Get a good night's sleep and I'll give you Rail Warrants in the morning and you can go home again. Goodnight".

Next morning we were given our rail warrants and ration cards and a warning that we could be recalled at 24 hours' notice and should not, therefore, stray far from the address we had given. A lorry was provided to carry us to the railway station and, once more, we were on our way home.

Each week I received, by mail, a ration card, an extension of my leave and a Post Office Draft for my pay. This went on until the 9th April, in all about nine weeks since I had left the ship in Glasgow. But all good things come to an end, as they say, and my disembarkation leave had been a good thing. I had seen my fiancée every day and it seemed as if we had never been apart.

When I finally returned to Kirton Lindsey I found myself attached to No.7 Secondary Flying School, whose role was to take newly-qualified pilots who had only just learned to fly solo in Tiger Moths, for the most part, and teach them to fly a more advanced aircraft, the North American Harvard. Whereas the Tiger Moth was a biplane, built from wood and canvas, with an open cockpit and fixed undercarriage, the Harvard was an all-metal monoplane, two cockpits in tandem, a retractable undercarriage and a much more powerful engine.

I was a Corporal, so I was given charge of two planes and a team of two engine mechanics and two airframe mechanics, in this instance, all members of the Women's Auxiliary Air Force, or 'Waafs', as they were usually called. I had never had the pleasure of working with women before, so it was to be a very new experience. Our main task was to carry out a daily serviceability check, refuel the aircraft and generally to ensure our aircraft were always ready for flight.

Normally, our planes would fly morning and afternoon and, sometimes, evening for night flying practice. The pilots were very young, perhaps nineteen or twenty in most cases, and their Instructors might be Commissioned Officers or Warrant Officers. So long as we did our jobs efficiently, everything went smoothly. I was very happy with my female team as they all co-operated and did a very good job for me.

Occasionally, if one of our aircraft was scheduled for Night Flying, the Instructor would take it up for a Night Flying Check in the afternoon. This consisted of a local flight of about thirty minutes, during which he would check that the aircraft was serviceable and fit to fly in the dark. When I got to know some of the instructors, I might be invited to accompany the instructor on this night flying check. I always accepted the invitation, as I enjoyed flying and hoped I might be invited to take control of the aircraft. One particular Warrant Officer, Don Green, used to take me up regularly and taught me to do turns and rolls, climbs and dives and, eventually, a loop-the-loop. One afternoon, as we were leaving the aircraft, he asked me if I had ever considered applying for pilot training. I had, in fact, volunteered before I left Halton some three years previously, but had heard nothing in reply. He offered to talk to the Chief Flying Instructor with a view to getting on a course. I agreed and thought no more of it.

Having heard nothing more about flying training, I volunteered for service abroad. Things were not going too well with Molly and I wanted a change of air. Not long afterwards, I was told that I was being posted to Singapore, so I put the idea of pilot training out of my mind.

My engagement to Molly had been showing signs of strain. I suppose the difference in our ages might have had some bearing on it. She, being four years older than me, understandably wanted to be married as soon as possible but I'm afraid I was rather immature and was, frankly, worried about the responsibility and expense. Although I had reached the exalted rank of Corporal, my pay was certainly not sufficient to support a wife. Molly was in a good job and could have kept on working but I did not fancy being a 'kept man'. To cut a long story short, I asked her to release me from my commitment and forget I existed. She was, naturally, very upset but we managed to part without blows and I went off to Singapore.

This posting overseas was very different from the last one. Once more at Burtonwood we were kitted out, this time with only tropical gear, and inoculated against the usual catalogue of diseases and then, all the corporals on the draft were separated from the others and shipped off to RAF Lyneham in Wiltshire, to be flown abroad. It seems our plane was not due to take off until the next day so we were accommodated at a Stately Home, called Bowood House. Next day we were back at Lyneham in good time to embark. This was to be my first experience of long-range air travel. Our aircraft was to be an Avro York, a development of the famous Lancaster Bomber. First impressions showed it to be a fairly comfortable aircraft with, being a high-wing monoplane, good visibility from all seats. I do not know whether it was for safety reasons but we were only to fly in daylight.

The first leg of our journey was from Lyneham to Malta, quite uneventful and we arrived fairly early. A friend and I, walking in Valetta at about 6.30pm, encountered two British sailors and asked one if he could direct us to a bar. He asked us to wait for his friend, who was buying a birthday card for his wife, and they would show us round the town. That was the commencement of the heaviest night I can ever remember, though, in truth, I remember very little of it. One thing I do recall is that those two sailors must have been at sea for a very long time for they would not allow us to spend a penny. Next day, badly hung over, we flew eastwards over the Mediterranean, without incident, until we reached the Levant Coast. This was near the end of 1947 and there was major trouble brewing in Palestine and Israel. As a precaution, the pilot took the plane up to about 17,000 feet. This was reckoned to be outside the Territorial Limits of the area and would have been fine but nobody told the passengers that they needed oxygen at that altitude.

After a time, the Navigator came aft and was greeted by half the passengers with severe headaches and some feeling very unwell. Immediately sensing what was wrong, he showed us how to deploy the oxygen masks and we were soon on the way to recovery. The flight continued and our next overnight stop was RAF Habbaniyah in the middle of the Iraqi desert. I have very little recollection of the place but that is not really surprising as these night stops were only for refuelling of humans and aircraft. I do recall one thing about our next stop at Karachi, where nobody was allowed to leave the aircraft until the whole plane, inside and out, had been fumigated. We sat on that tarmac in blazing heat, with all doors closed, for about half-an-hour whilst the natives came in and sprayed everything, by which time we were all ready to melt. As the sprayers disappeared, an RAF policeman walked through the plane and, noticing the near-forest of Corporals' stripes, asked if we were all police. In chorus we all replied, "Not on your B****y life!" I think he got the message.

The next leg took us to Columbo, Ceylon (Sri Lanka) where we were to sleep in wooden huts and must use the mosquito nets provided. When the time came for turning in I went round my bed and religiously tucked the edge of my net under the mattress. As I rolled under the net to get into bed, I looked up towards the ceiling. By the head of my bed was a post, supporting the roof, and, just disappearing into the space between post and roof, was the biggest spider I have ever seen. It was black and very hairy and its legs must have been at least six inches long. Believe me, I tucked in the rest of my net VERY carefully.

Next day, the final stage of our journey, from Ceylon to Singapore, was the longest leg of all. It took just short of nine hours, all over the sea, making the full journey just about forty hours flying in five days.

14. Singapore Interlude

We landed at Tengah, on the island, and were taken, by lorry of course, to a transit camp on the Malayan Peninsula called, I believe, Sembuang, where we stayed for a day or two, whilst our postings were decided. Eventually I was sent to Changi (now an International Airport) on the eastern side of the island. On reaching Changi, I was directed to the barrack block which housed 84 Squadron and told to unpack my kit and then lose myself for twenty-four hours. The date was 20th October 1947, the wedding day of Princess Elizabeth and Prince Philip. There had been a parade that morning and the rest of the day was free in celebration. I spent the rest of the day finding my way around the place and was pleased to discover that the ground floor of our barrack block was the Malcolm Club. During World War II, a group of four brothers were enlisted in the RAF and all became aircrew in Bomber Command. One by one they were all killed in action. Their mother, Lady Malcolm, donated money to build clubs, open to all ranks, on RAF stations. These were social clubs with bars and other leisure facilities and were very popular. Changi's club was the ground floor of our block, we were on the first floor and the top floor was the Station Dance Hall.

No.84 Squadron was formed in England, in, I believe, 1917 and after a very few months was posted overseas, where it remained, in various locations, throughout its existence. When I joined the squadron in 1947 it was equipped with Bristol Beaufighters, which were designated as 'fighter/bombers' and sizeable aircraft, weighing some eleven tons. They flew in the latter years of the war and had some success against the German pilotless flying bombs. Their main purpose in Malaya was to patrol the west coast, ostensibly monitoring weather conditions. Singapore has the reputation of having a temperature range between 70-80 degrees Fahrenheit, fine sunny mornings and rain every afternoon. No doubt this is generalisation and therefore liable to question but in my short experience it was not too far from the truth.

About two months after my arrival, one of our aircraft, returning from patrol, found the island had disappeared. It was, in fact, sitting, soaking, under a dense bank of cloud which was dumping rain on the island at a record rate. The plane, flown by our Squadron Commander, circled at a distance until, with fuel almost gone, the pilot had no recourse but to make a forced landing on a nearby island. In fact the landing was made offshore in shallow water. No-one was hurt but, I suspect, the aircraft was a write-off. The crew were rescued by boat, the next day. Another of our aircraft was taken into the hangar for routine servicing when it was discovered that its fuel tanks were perforated by corrosion. An urgent inspection of the other aircraft showed them to be in, almost, the same condition. The whole squadron was immediately grounded pending a supply of new tanks. It was subsequently discovered that the aircraft had, at some not too distant date, been in storage, in the open, somewhere up country in the jungle, where the heat and very high humidity had corroded the metal skins of the tanks. All war planes, at that time, had what were called self-sealing tanks. The tanks were sheathed in a layer of foam rubber which, if contaminated by petrol, would swell. Thus, if in action a tank was pierced by bullets, the fuel would swell the rubber which, in turn, would swell and seal the holes. In the case of our Beau-fighters, the corrosion, invisible to normal servicing procedures, had the same effect as bullets. Supplies of replacement tanks would take some time to be delivered from the UK and, in the meantime, there was a squadron, grounded, and with no aircraft. Most of the pilots were immediately sent back to England to collect replacement planes so they could, at least, keep up their flying practise. In the event, the replacements turned out to be Harvards, which had to be flown, in short stages, from England to Singapore. It was a very slow journey. The replacements eventually arrived, were checked over and normal service was resumed.

Even the most qualified pilots are required to fly a certain number of hours per month and perform a set number of take-offs and landings, to keep their flying licence valid. The Harvard, being a two-seater, there was plenty of opportunity for ground staff to get a ride. I had my share and more.

One day I was called in to see the Squadron Commander unexpectedly. He had, apparently, received a letter from RAF Records Office concerning me. They demanded to know why I had volunteered for posting overseas without waiting for the reply to my application for aircrew training. Fortunately, I was able to convince my boss that I had not applied for such training but that the Chief Flying Instructor at Kirton Lindsey may well have done so in my name. The Squadron Leader accepted my explanation and asked if I would still be interested in a flying career. I said I would like to try it and I was then sent back to work.

Some time later, I was called to the Station Sick Bay for a medical examination, which I believe was successful. Due to someone's inefficiency, I was called for that exam several times.

Each time I passed with flying colours and, eventually, the results were despatched to the UK. The next thing I heard was that I was to return to the UK for Aircrew Aptitude Tests.

The tests were to be carried out at North Weald in Essex but, first, I went to RAF Driffield in east Yorkshire until North Weald was ready to test me. At Driffield I was employed on servicing de Havilland Mosquitoes, twin engine aircraft made largely of wood. Driffield was another flying school though more advanced than my previous experience. I was there for only about two months before being called to North Weald. During that two-month period, I was called upon to participate in the annual Air Officer's Inspection of the station, a routine examination of the work and record of the station by a senior officer. It involves the station in a lot of extra work since it is an examination of the Station Commanders' efficiency.

The troops have to take part in a Ceremonial Parade and, traditionally, the day is rounded off by a flypast of some of the station's aircraft and I was fortunate enough to be invited to fly, as passenger, in one of the Squadron's Mosquitos, by far the fastest aircraft I had flown in to date. As we crossed the airfield, at very low altitude, I happened to notice that the altimeter was registering a negative height. I asked the pilot if he normally flew underground on these occasions. He laughed and said he had not bothered to recalibrate the altimeter as he knew we would only be flying locally and visually, rather than by instruments.

15. Misemployment

At North Weald I was put through all kinds of tests, height, weight, hearing, sight, all were tested, not to mention the usual 'sample' in a bottle. There were tests to determine colour blindness, aptitude for Morse Code, handling of controls such as the control column. Eventually it was all over and I was accepted. The next stop, believe it or not, was Kirton Lindsey, which was now non-flying and a holding unit to make up the numbers for the next course. I began to feel that Kirton was my natural home. When our group reached its quota of twenty pupils, we moved on to RAF Wittering, near Stamford in Lincolnshire.

I was a member of No.20 course, which, coincidentally, had 20 members and was planned to last 20 weeks. On the evening of our arrival, we were assembled to be addressed by the Commanding Officer. He told us something about the course and stressed how intensive it would be. We must be prepared to work very hard and to spend our evenings revising the work we had done that day.

"Your revision should not be left to the last week of the course but should start on the first day," was his mantra.

Our course was composed of some eight or nine chaps who, like me, had been several years in the service; the remainder had spent some years in the Air Training Corps. In short, we all knew the basics of Air Force life, the marching and manoeuvring on a parade ground. It transpired that, in four weeks' time, there was to be an AOC's (Air Officer Commanding) Inspection.

During the first week of the course, several lectures were cancelled so that we could be taken on the parade ground and taught how to stand to attention, stand at ease, turn left or right at the halt. In other words, the very basic points of drill with which we were all more than familiar. In addition, the usual weekly inspection of our accommodation was carried out nightly. This involved not only the thorough cleaning of the rooms each evening but also standing by our beds for inspection at about ten o'clock each night.

There was no time for revision, even if we had something to revise, unless we were prepared to stay up until the small hours of the morning. Many of the senior entries, who were close to the end of their course, did stay up, after cleaning and inspection, to catch up with their revision until four or five o'clock in the morning.

Two of us decided this was not what we volunteered for and decided to leave. We submitted our resignations from the course, and asked to be returned to our former trades as we were not sufficiently dedicated to becoming aircrew. Our resignations were accepted, almost without question, and we packed our kit and went to the Aircrew Allocation Unit (AAU) at RAF Innsworth, near Gloucester.

AAU was a small unit to which, aircrew surplus to a squadrons allocation, returning from courses or renewing their service commitments were sent to be re-allocated to new duties. Whilst we were there we were employed on "pass time" jobs. In other words, people were employed to keep us occupied until our future was decided. Some days we were taken on the parade ground and made to drill each other from opposite sides of the square. At other times we might be given gardening jobs to clean up the gardens around the office buildings. On rare occasions we were sent on Escape and Evasion Exercises. On one of these occasions I was told to make my way to Newport in south Wales and make myself known to the landlord of the King's Head Hotel. He would supply me with proof of having been there and then I could return to Innsworth. Fortunately, it was a fine, sunny day and I quite enjoyed my trip. I had the opportunity to glance at a map before I left so I had some idea of the direction I should travel. I suppose I left Innsworth at around nine-thirty and arrived in Newport soon after one o'clock. I had been very lucky with hitch-hiking lifts. Reporting to the hostelry, I was greeted by the landlord, who, it seemed had a friend at Innsworth. He not only gave me proof of arrival but sat me down to lunch and a pint. What a shame we did not have more of these exercises!

Fortunately, we had plenty of time for sport and I was happy to play football at every opportunity. One or two of the officers of AAU enjoyed "the beautiful game" too and would turn out with us for a game. I actually had a trial for the Innsworth station team. I had a reasonable game but, probably blotted my copy book when an attempted clearance skidded off my head into my team's goal.

One fine, warm day, I was detailed to tidy up the grass and flower-bed around the unit office building. Not an onerous job but, in the warm conditions, I could get too warm. Little did I or anyone else, realise how that day's work was to affect my life. As I pottered away with a pair of shears and a hand rake, a window above my head was flung open and a girl's head and shoulders leaned out. We looked at each other and she asked what I was doing. We said hello and that was the start of a romance which went on and on. Yes, we fell in love and were married three months later. Many thought they knew the reason for the rush and many more said it would never last. Wrong on both counts. Our first child was born 369 days after the wedding and the marriage was still strong fifty-eight years later. The reason for the rushed marriage was because Joan had been warned that she would be leaving for Egypt. At that time married women were not allowed to be members of the WAAF. So, we got married.

After I had been at Innsworth about seven or eight weeks, I, and my colleague, was called for an interview with two of the officers. The interviews started very formally and were arranged to try to determine why I, and many others, were opting out from their aircrew training at Wittering. After my interview, my colleague went in and his reasons were examined. We were then asked to wait in the corridor outside for several minutes before being called in together. This time, someone had been busy on the phone because there were four cups and saucers on the table along with a large pot of tea. We were asked to sit down and a very informal interview took place. All the papers from the first interview had been sent out and we were asked to give our real reasons for resigning from the course.

We both gave our views on the totally unfair and unnecessary hardships and gave our opinions on who was to blame. It seemed there had been a significant number of drop-outs and the Air Ministry was worried, not least over the unnecessary expense of calling in good candidates from all over the world, only to have them drop out prematurely. We heard, much later, that there had been several staff changes at Wittering and things seemed to be going much more smoothly. One thing we were both asked in our interview was whether we thought we needed a refresher course before returning to our former trades. We both agreed this would not be necessary provided we were not kept too long at Innsworth. Whether or not this was the correct answer was never made clear to us, but I was never again employed as an Engine Fitter, my basic trade.

From Innsworth, I was posted to an Armament Training School at Kirkham, near Blackpool, where I was employed as a store man in the Motor Transport Servicing Section. Far from being employed in my own trade, there was not a single aircraft on the station. I would make fortnightly trips southwards to see my new girlfriend and before long we were engaged to be married. It was then we heard that Joan had been warned for service overseas. We appealed against the posting on the grounds that we were to be married at Christmas. The appeal was allowed and we breathed a little more freely.

Our wedding took place at the Church of the Ascension, in Romford, Essex, where Joan's family lived, on the 27th December 1948. It was a terribly foggy day and there were just thirteen people in the church. Some friends we had invited could not get there at all and one or two arrived very late. But we were there, the vicar was there and with the necessary witnesses we were wed.

By March, I had been misemployed for the statutory six months and I applied for a posting on those grounds. There was a need for people with a knowledge of German to train as interpreters. I had studied German and French at school and had applied for the course and was waiting for a reply. As luck would have it, the results of both applications came at the same time. I was to report to the Air Ministry for interview, and, on the very same day, I was to report to RAF Halton, Buckingham-shire, on posting. I decided to go to Romford, Joan's home, and drop my kit then go to Air Ministry for their interview. I then proposed to stay the night at Romford and carry on to Halton the following day. At the Air Ministry there were, it seemed, hundreds of applicants, some of whom, I heard, were real linguists already. One chap spoke fluently in five European languages, others had two or three languages. I did not expect to be successful. After the interview, with no clue as to the results, I went back to Romford , collected my kit and, the following day, went on to Halton.

16. Gliding Along

I arrived very nervously at Halton, since it was, after all, still No.1 School of Technical Training and I had been misemployed for about twelve months. I felt sure I was being drafted in as an Instructor of Apprentices. I need not have worried. The first office I found booked me in and told me to report to Station Flight at the airfield. This Flight had about three aircraft for Communications and to give flight experience to the Apprentices. At Station Flight office I was told to take myself to the Air Traffic Control building and ask to see Flt Lt Walker. Off I went, full of apprehension. I had been here in wartime but, now, it seemed, apprentices were given the chance to learn to fly gliders. Flight Lieutenant Walker was the officer in charge of the Apprentices Glider Flight. This was all very fine and proper, but where did I fit in as an Engine Fitter on a Glider Flight? I soon found out that the gliders in question were launched into the air by a tow from a cable driven by a winch, or by a tow from a light aircraft. In this case the winch was the method in use. I was to be trained as a winch operator to replace Flight Sergeant Inglis, who was coming to the end of his service career.

Winch operating sounds a rather boring, sedentary occupation but there were to be times when life became somewhat more exciting. We had, if I remember rightly, four Slingsby Cadet gliders, one Dagling and one Kranich high performance sail-plane. At the time I thought Dagling might be the German word for duckling, but my German-English dictionary does not list the word. Redundant Balloon Winches were used to launch the gliders, one had an integral prime mover and the other was a trailer type unit. Four Willys Jeeps were used to retrieve gliders on the ground. These were later superseded by two Bedford 15cwt pick-up trucks.

The primary trainer was the Dagling, a rather primitive glider having a large bulky wing under which was slung a substantial keel on which was mounted a seat. A rudder, attached at the rear was operated by wires from a foot-bar in front of the seat. The Dagling was never towed very quickly and, apart from the Apprentice, carried several well-filled sandbags on its keel to ensure that it did not leave the ground. Towed along the ground, the Apprentice would try to keep the wings level and keep the nose pointing towards the winch. Once he had mastered this art, he could be moved on to the Cadet, single-seater for what we called the 'Airborne Slide' phase. Once more the pupil had to learn to keep the craft straight and level and then he would be encouraged to ease the control column back gently, which caused the craft to leave the ground to a height of eight to ten feet, then ease the column forward to gently land on the ground. If this had been managed in a sufficiently short distance, he might try a second lift-off. The vast majority of pupils managed this drill quite quickly and successfully but, inevitably, a few would become over-excited and actually faint. When this happened the winch-operator came into his own. If a pilot fainted he would tend to slump in his seat and the weight of his arm might push the control column over to one side, so the glider veered off course, at an angle to the tow-line. By careful use of the throttle and clutch, the winch man must try to bring the glider back on course and gradually reduce its speed so it returned to earth without damage. A clumsy jerk on the tow-line could cause the plane to turn sharply, generating extra lift on one wing with the result that the glider could flip over and land upside-down. This would not be good for the pilot or the glider. In the course of some twelve months on the glider flight, I suppose I experienced four or five such incidents and am pleased to say they all passed off successfully.

When the Apprentices had shown themselves capable of taking off and landing in a straight line, it was time for them to experience real flying. Initially, circuits and landings were flown accompanied by Flt Lt Walker. For this exercise, from the winch man's point of view, the aim was to provide a smooth uptake followed by rapid initial acceleration then gradually reducing tow speed as the craft gained altitude. At the very top of the climb the pilot would dip the nose slightly and operate the cable release. The winch operator would then speed up the winch, as the cable fell, to avoid tangles.

During this phase of activities, accidents were, fortunately, rare but potentially spectacular. On one occasion, when the glider was well into the climb, the cable broke. Fortunately, the flight was accompanied and the instructor was able to retrieve the situation and land safely. On another occasion, when I happened to be on leave, an even rarer accident happened. The Ford V8 engine on the winch seized, during the climb, and no less than three connecting rods came through the side of the engine sump. Needless to say, the engine was written off but, once again, the glider landed safely. My time as a Winch Operator proved to be more exciting than I had expected but it was an interesting period nevertheless.

The result of my interpreter interview came though around the end of June that year. It seemed I had been accepted and was to be posted to Hamburg University for the course. Flight Lieutenant Walker was rather upset, as I had just been classified as a qualified Winch Operator and, if I left, it might take him six months to train someone else. To cut a long story short, he contacted the Station Commander, who was very keen to keep the glider flight in action, and my posting was cancelled. I was a bit disappointed though not entirely unhappy, because we had just realised that Joan and my first joint production was on the way. My posting to Germany would have entailed a separation of a year at just the wrong stage of our marriage.

The following year, 1950, was something of a crisis year. Joan was living with her parents and conditions were rather cramped. She had three sisters and a brother, who, at the time were changing their situations. The eldest sister was married and had a child and was hoping to move out into her own housing. The brother was due to be demobilised after serving a time in the Army. The youngest sister was still at school and Mother was about to be admitted to hospital for a major operation. Joan had a new baby and things were beginning to pile up on her. The Soldiers', Airmens' and Sailors' Families association advised me to apply for a Compassionate Posting nearer home.

The posting was granted and I was posted to RAF Chigwell, just three miles from home. Was I going from the frying pan into the fire? Chigwell was the home of the RAF Central Trade Test Board. Was I expected to return to Engine Fitting as an Examiner? I need not have worried, as a lowly corporal I was to be just a "dogsbody".

I was fully informed on my first day at Chigwell when I was interviewed by an Engineering Officer. He greeted me at interview with the words, "I believe you are an ex-Halton apprentice?" I replied in the affirmative. "Good," he said." So you can do just about anything. Do you see that window behind you? Outside is a flap which I can raise or lower if the sun is in my eyes. The string is broken and I would like you to repair it".

The task took all of five minutes and he then directed me to the Sports Field. I was to join a team of four men, headed by a Flight Sergeant, who were building a Cricket Pavilion. I joined them and we worked well together, in spite of being Aircraft Tradesmen. We finished off the roof then started work inside on heating and lighting systems and it shaped up very well. When we had nearly completed the task, the Station Commander came to inspect our work. He seemed very pleased and almost amicable. When he remarked on the high standard of work, I cheekily said, "I agree and I'm thinking of moving my family in at the weekend." A very cheeky joke but it was taken as meant. I am sure he never knew that two of us Corporals had been leaving off work at about four o'clock to help a local farmer harvest his corn.

Later, somebody allowed all the RAF policemen to be demobilised without asking for replacements. The Guardroom must not be left unmanned so three of us, all corporals, were given the task of manning the guard room, day and night for six weeks. It was not a terribly hard task but, if one of us wanted a day off the others must cover his shift. It became very tiring.

17. A Change of Direction

By now I was resigned to the fact that I was no longer required as an Engine Fitter and, as there appeared to be a shortage of Electrical Fitters, I applied for a Conversion Course. I was accepted and posted to RAF Melksham in Wiltshire. My decision to change trades was a hard one. I had dreamed of being an Engine Fitter for a good part of my life. The cause of my dilemma was not simply because I had been misemployed for so long. There was a surplus of personnel in many aircraft trades. During the recent war thousands of conscripts had been admitted to the Service, learned a trade, enjoyed the life and had decided to sign on as Regulars in the RAF. Most of these had been promoted quickly to fill the losses due to casualties. As a result, younger people, many like myself, who had been serving overseas when the war ended found that the Promotion Ladder was already fully occupied. We could continue to serve in the lower ranks, possibly, like me, misemployed, or we could try another route to the Sergeants Mess. I talked it over with Joan's father, who had encountered a similar problem in his life after the First World War. In my case, it came down to a choice of Electrical Fitter or Radar Fitter. I decided that Electrics would be better and was, in any case, the basis of all such trades.

18. Father-in-Law

Joan's father was a stocky chap about 5ft 6ins tall. He was born in 1887 to a newly-widowed mother. As a teenager he completed an apprenticeship in an Engineering situation. When World War I started he joined the Army and served in the Royal Horse Artillery Regiment in France all through the war. He reached the rank of Sergeant and fought in many of the major battles of the war but would never talk about his experiences in any detail. Some of the younger members of his family never knew that he had been wounded in action but I noticed that, on occasions, particularly in damp weather, he developed a limp in his left leg, although I never found out the precise nature of the injury; he would not tell.

When he returned to civilian life he could not find employment and, after a frustrating period of unemployment, he decided to become a wood-worker. Typically, he decided to start at the bottom and took himself off to Hull where he knew much of the nation's timber was imported. Having learned as much as he could about raw timber, he found employment with a firm who would teach him how to work with wood. For most of his working life, he was employed in the East End of London by a firm who took on all kinds of woodwork. He learned to do repair work on buildings, how to make furniture and, during World War II, he learned to repair bomb damage and joined the Home Guard.

When, eventually, he met and married his wife Lizzie, they lived in Hackney, East London. When their family out-grew their small flat, he moved them out to Romford, but first he made much of the furniture they would need in their new home. He made two double beds, one single, a dining suite along with two sideboards, bookcases and many other things, all with his own two hands at his firm's premises after normal business hours. He was a remarkable man who taught me a lot.

When he learned that I wanted to marry his daughter Joan, he asked me to join him in his dining room. As I entered the room he said, "I believe you want to marry my daughter?"

"Yes," I said.

"Thank Gawd for that!" he said. "I thought I was stuck with that one!" We both laughed and had a drink together.

19. Career Changes

To get back to my Service career, when I reported to RAF Melksham I learned that I would be able to take an Electrical Mechanics' Course, followed by a Fitters' Course (provided that I passed the first one, of course). The two courses together would take a year, with a short break in between them.

During the first course I worked fairly hard, though I did not find it difficult. During this period the RAF adopted a new procedure. There was always a shortage of Married Quarters for non-commissioned ranks but it was decided that if a married airman could reasonably expect to spend twelve months at a Training School, he would be allowed to apply for Married Quarters at that school. I applied and was allocated a house during my retraining. We had never previously had a chance to occupy a married quarter and had only seen one type of quarter, a pre-war type at Halton. Pre-war quarters were very small, of really basic style and usually terraced houses. Joan had not been impressed with what she had seen. When we took over our new home at Melksham, she arrived, with our first-born Susan, after dark and with no idea what to expect. The house was semi-detached, almost new, with two bedrooms, kitchen, dining room, sitting room, bathroom, toilet and garden. My wife was absolutely delighted and so was I. We soon settled in and were very happy in that house.

When I successfully completed my training, I fully expected to be posted to some distant outpost, but no, they asked me to stay on at Melksham as an instructor on the Mechanics Course.

Naturally, I think, I was a bit apprehensive, not having worked on, or even seen an aircraft as an Electrician but, after a two-week course on how to instruct (at RAF Cosford) I was considered competent and went back to Melksham and 'in at the deep end', so to speak. I continued as an Instructor until about April, 1953, with reasonable success, until I was posted to RAF St Athan in South Wales, my first posting to that country.

St Athan was a Maintenance Unit where men worked, just like being in a factory, on benches, stripping and rebuilding electrical components from eight till five, five days a week. By this time I had been promoted to Sergeant and was told to set up a production line to repair Electrical Voltage Regulators. I was given the Spare Parts Catalogue and told to order all the spares needed to service and rebuild "x" number of regulators. I had no experience of such a task and, it seemed, there was no help available. I took the job in hand and ordered every spare I could find in the book in lavish quantities. My demands went off to the appropriate depot and we awaited results.

I am afraid I never found out whether my demands had been inspired or diabolical because Records Office, in their impenetrable wisdom, decided at this point that I should have another spell of foreign service. I was posted to Iraq and, in particular, to RAF Habbaniyah.

20. RAF Habbaniyah

At this point I feel I must devote a little space to Habbaniyah.

"Of all Royal Air Force bases Habbaniyah is, perhaps, the most remarkable." So wrote Dennis Richards in "The Flight at Odds" Volume 1 of The Royal Air Force 1939-1945.

Under the terms of the Anglo-Iraq treaty of 1930, the British were allowed a base on Iraqi soil, west of the Euphrates. This was to be Habbaniyah, 50 miles west of Baghdad, carefully situated at a bend of the river Euphrates. Building was commenced in 1934 and the camp was occupied in 1937.

By 1941 there were about 1,200 British airmen at Habbaniyah, along with six companies of native Levies, four Assyrian and two Iraqis. In addition, there were the Levies' families, the bearers, labourers and dhobis and all their families, in all about 9,000 men, women and children, who were housed in the Civil Cantonment. The Levies had been raised to help maintain order in the period 1922-30, when the RAF was responsible for the internal security of Iraq. They were retained, later, to protect RAF bases in the area.

Of material comforts, Habbaniyah had everything. Situated in the middle of a desert, scattered about with occasional clumps of camel-thorn, Habbaniyah appeared like a gleaming green jewel set against the golden background of sand. The planners had not failed to realise that, with sufficient water, the desert of Iraq can be made to blossom into life – hence the riverside site and the extensive irrigation system. Verdant lawns surrounded the buildings and the twenty-eight miles of roads within the camp were lined with trees – date palms, eucalyptus trees and pomegranate bushes. Within the camp the extensive Command Gardens were laid out. Here grew flowers and plants of every description in abundance, from the most exotic cactus to the lowly daffodil. Clematis, honeysuckle, jasmine, lilac and bougainvillea, all were there. Orange, banana, lime and fig grew alongside the more familiar apple, pear and plum. Snowdrops appeared in their season and London Pride grew all around.

Habbaniyah had its own Electric Power Station, with capacity enough for a small town, its own water purification plant and extensive cold storage depot. The Station Farm bred pigs and cattle for fresh meat and milk. The camp's sewage treatment plant was situated a short distance downstream.

Levant Command Headquarters, which administered about 10 stations in the Middle East, was situated at Habbaniyah, as was a fully equipped hospital. The camp administration was divided into Flying Wing, Station Headquarters, Supply Wing and Transit Wing, each having its own Officers', Senior NCOs, and Airmen's Messes. The Hospital and Air Headquarters were similarly served and were independently administered.

In each of these locations various activities were organised for the off-duty entertainment of the inhabitants. Forces Radio Station Habbaniyah broadcast for up to 80 hours per week, manned by volunteers. The programme consisted of relayed BBC News, when reception was good enough, interspaced with music programmes of requests and announcers' choice. There was a fine gymnasium, indoor and outdoor cinemas and the finest swimming pool in the RAF – outdoor of course. Numerous football and cricket pitches were provided and no fewer than 56 tennis courts. Quite close to the camp entrance and inside the perimeter, was a nine-hole golf course and, alongside the horse race-course were riding stables where, for very little money, an airman could have a part-share in a horse and ride twice a week. The Habbaniyah Hunt had its own pack of hounds and there was a full-sized Polo Ground.

Within the camp were two small shopping precincts, known locally as Cheapside and Little Cheapside, where one could purchase food and drink, have a haircut or order made-to-measure clothing. All the camp roads had names like Kingsway, Piccadilly, Cranwell Avenue and other names reminiscent of England, home and the RAF.

Habbaniyah had three magnificent stone-built churches to cater for the spiritual needs of Church of England, Roman Catholic and non-Conformist Creeds.

Everything, then, was done to make Habbaniyah the most pleasant prison that human ingenuity could devise. For prison it was, with its seven-mile perimeter fence enclosed by an eight-foot un-climbable fence. Outside the fence there was – NOTHING – except the lake and an occasional visit to the dreary arcades and overpriced delights of Baghdad.

The lake is worthy of mention, being man-made. It is a large lake, many square miles in area. It was created some years before the Second World War as a flood control measure. Each Spring, as the snow melts on the Turkish mountains, water would surge down the Euphrates, causing severe flooding downstream. To relieve this flooding a canal was created to divert excess water into a natural depression, forming a lake. Thus the danger of flooding was greatly reduced and later, when the river levels had reduced, water could be released from the lake and back into the river.

For several years between the two World Wars, Empire Airways and British Overseas Airways used the lake as a Staging

Post to refuel their Flying Boats en route to India and places East. When the airways changed their routes, following developments which eliminated the need to refuel there, the Airways moved out from the lake and the terminal buildings were offered, on permanent loan, to RAF Habbaniyah. A Rest and Leave Centre was established where personnel could find a very comfortable retreat where they could rest, swim or fish in the lake or, perhaps sail one of the Fireflies from the nearby Habbaniyah Sailing Club.

Such, then, was this perfect prison. The inmates' sentiments are aptly summed up in Habbaniyah's theme song – author unknown.

> Sweet music rising to the sky,
> In tune with songbirds fluttering by.
> A garden fair where all is bliss,
> A place the air force would not miss.
> To passers-by it thus appears,
> To us inside – Two Bloody Years!

The fence had the dual purpose of keeping camp personnel and the natives in and animals of the desert out. This was important in view of the camp's isolated position 300 miles from the nearest British Base on the Persian Gulf and 500 miles from Palestine. Habbaniyah would be in grave danger if the Political Climate in Baghdad changed. On the north and east, the river offered some protection, on the west was open sand. To the south, beyond the airfield, rose a plateau some 200 feet high. And here, on the morning of 30th April 1941, there were assembled 9,000 Iraqi Troops with 28 pieces of artillery.

Raschid Ali, an Iraqi politician of chequered career, aided by four Generals, had seized power on April 3rd. The Regent had fled to Habbaniyah and was flown to Basra for shipment, in a British ship, to Transjordan.

On April 16th Raschid Ali was informed of our intention to move military forces along Iraqi lines of communication. On April 18th a contingent of British and Indian troops disembarked at Basra. At the same time 400 men of the King's Own Regiment were flown from Karachi to Shaibah by 31 Squadron. Two more ships, with ancillary troops, were due to land at Basra on 28th April. Raschid Ali refused them permission to land until the main contingent had moved out of Iraq. On April 29th the new arrivals disembarked.

By the afternoon of the same day, the political temperature in Baghdad had reached fever heat and it was felt advisable to move all British dependants from the city. Two hundred and thirty women and children were moved from Baghdad to Habbaniyah in lorries. Here then, was the situation. Twelve hundred officers and men of the RAF, 230 women and children, six companies of Levies, 9,000 native men, women and children, were in this perfect, self-contained prison in the middle of a desert. All these, menaced, at a range of one thousand yards, by 9,000 enemy troops with 28 pieces of artillery. For protection – there were no operational units on the station.

Habbaniyah was the home of No.4 Flying School. Since April 5th the workshops and hangars had echoed to the sound of ground crews fitting bomb racks to trainer aircraft. By April 30th about 70 aircraft had been converted, of which about 60 were Audaxes and Oxfords. The Oxford was a twin-engined monoplane whilst the Audax, an ex-operational machine of 1930 vintage, was an adaptation of the Hawker Hart bomber. It had, an addition, a hinged arm for picking up messages, hence its popular description "an 'art wiv an 'ook".

These Audaxes were modified to carry two 250lb bombs in place of their "official" load of twenty-pounders. The Oxford was never intended to carry armament of any kind but was given an ingenious fitment for eight 20lb bombs with their tail-fins protruding below the fuselage. Six Gladiators were sent from Egypt to join the three training fighters at Habbaniyah.

Intensive courses in bomb-aiming and air gunnery had been started. Few of the pilots had operational experience, some of them belonged to the Royal Hellenic Air Force and some were unsuitable for operational duties – for various reasons. In all thirty-five qualified pilots were mustered and the more promising pupils were "promoted" to swell the total. The remaining pupils and volunteer ground staff were employed as observers and gunners, for, of these, only four qualified practitioners could be found.

This "Fred Karno's Air Force" became known as 'The Habbaniyah Strike Force' – four bombing squadrons and one flight of Gladiators. The runways at Habbaniyah were outside the perimeter fence so the golf course and polo ground were combined to make a landing ground for Audaxes within the fence. This necessitated the felling of trees, obliterating roads and filling in of bunkers.

No.1 Company of RAF Regiment Armoured cars and 400 men of the KORR were flown in from Shaibah on April 24th.

The camp held full rations for only 12 days and was crammed full of non-combatants. It was exposed on all sides and a single hit might demolish the water tower or the power station and cripple resistance. Few small arms were available and no artillery. Correction: two small field pieces, of 1914-18 vintage, used as decoration outside the Aircraft Depot, were pressed into service and crews and ammunition were flown in.

The loyalty of the Levies might be questionable, they were, after all, Iraqis. In fact, this proved not to be the case.

Meanwhile, the enemy forces were growing. All targets within range had been catalogued by photographic mosaics. On 1st May more guns were counted.

No message had, as yet, been received from London. Then a message arrived:

"The position of Habbaniyah must be restored and the enemy forced to retire".

Ten Wellington bombers were flown in from Egypt to Shaibah, in case they were needed. A further message was received from Winston Churchill, then Prime Minister:

"If you must strike, Strike hard!"

At first light on May 2nd, No 4 Flying School went into action. They were airborne at 0445 hours and Wellingtons, from Shaibah, dropped the first bombs at 0500 hours. As the Wellingtons turned for home, 35 Audaxes, Gordons and Oxfords went into action. They dived down to 1,000 feet to be sure of their targets. One instructor pilot and two pupils were killed when their Oxford was shot down in flames. Another instructor, in an Audax, took three bullets in his shoulder and slumped down over his joystick. His pupil, though wounded himself, hauled him back into his seat and persuaded him to land the aircraft, with one hand, before fainting away again.

A Wellington was badly hit and forced landed at Habbaniyah where it stood in the thick of the enemies' fire. A mechanic drove out on a tractor, flanked by armoured cars, and had just fixed a rope round the tail-wheel when shells hit the aircraft and tractor. The driver just got clear, in an armoured car, before tractor and aircraft became airborne on a cloud of high explosive.

By 10am the enemy guns were quite subdued but Raschid Ali's aircraft, quite as numerous as Habbaniyah's and backed by far more operational equipment, now appeared on the scene. They turned out to be far less formidable than the guns, which were rather dangerous. Apart from the incessant din of shrapnel clattering on the corrugated iron hangar roofs, which was disconcerting, there was always the danger of an "accidental" hit.

If legend is to be believed, only a pair of storks nesting on the roof of Air Headquarters and the Station Warrant Officer remained completely unperturbed. The storks remained on the wireless mast until their two youngsters crashed trying to be prematurely airborne. One was seized and devoured by a jackal. The other broke a wing and expired when it found itself in the Station Hospital about to be X-rayed. The Station Warrant Officer is alleged to have stuck his head out of a shelter in time to see an airman bolting for cover.

"Now then, my man," he cried. "Pull up your stockings and don't run around so slovenly!"

The Iraqis' aim was poor, their hearts were obviously not on the job. Neither the water tower nor the power station were hit, nor were many aircraft on the ground. Oxfords and Gordons were taking off in full view of the gunners. They would start their engines behind the hangars then accelerate out, through the gate and off in a steep banking turn, climbing away from the plateau. Meanwhile, Audaxes from the polo ground would harass the gunners with well-aimed bombs. By this means, even Douglasses and Valentias got away with women and children for Shaibah and safety.

A second flight of Wellingtons, of 37 Squadron, arrived at Shaibah from Egypt. More fighting had now broken out in Southern Iraq but the situation there was not so critical as at Habbaniyah.

By nightfall on that first day, the Habbaniyah Striking Force had flown 193 sorties for the loss of two machines in the air and three on the ground. Ground crews worked all night to service aircraft – including a Wellington stranded on the runway. A quiet night passed but, with the first light came more shells.

This was the pattern until the night of 5th/6th May, when, for no apparent reason, the enemy "folded his tents and stole away in the night". Reconnaissance at first light found the plateau empty.

Armoured cars and infantry set off in pursuit and a sharp encounter followed in which the Audaxes joined. The enemy was pushed back beyond Sin el Dhibban. This was an important achievement for at Sin el Dhibban was the main pumping station for Habbaniyah's sewage treatment works. The enemy seemed to have overlooked this for the pumping station kept working throughout the siege. So, as always, one could have the satisfaction of "pulling the chain" all through the crisis, a rare privilege overseas.

During the afternoon, aircraft reported a large column of troops coming up from Fallujah. This column was attacked by 40 pilots near Sin el Dhibban. The last pilot to attack reported that, as he turned away, he saw a solid mass of flames 250 yards long, barbed by flashes of exploding ammunition. Raschid Ali's forces were completely routed and he himself expelled from Iraq. Life quietened down and the Regent returned to Baghdad.

A storm in a teacup, did you say? Not so! This incident could have changed the whole course of the war. On May 13th a

Blenheim aircraft was attacked by a Messerschmitt 110 over Mosul, a city in the north of Iraq. The Germans were desperately short of oil and would dearly like to have a foothold in Iraq. Their plans, however, received another severe setback. A Heinkel aircraft, of German origin, carrying Major Axel von Blomberg, flew in to land at Baghdad Airport, hoping to take part in a conference to secure oil supplies. A few trigger-happy tribesmen loosed off some pot-shots. The result was that, when the reception party met the aircraft, they found, not the vigorous advisor and co-ordinator they had expected, but a very dead German with a bullet in his head. Thus the German attempt to negotiate for oil came to an inauspicious end.

21. Life in the Desert

Life at Habbaniyah quickly returned to normal and a quiet time was had by all, until the Military Coup in 1958 – but that is another story.

My arrival at Habbaniyah was in September 1953 and, as a Sergeant, I was put in charge of the Electrical Section of the Aircraft Servicing Flight. I had one Corporal and a couple of Electrical Mechanics and a section consisting of a small Common Room and an even smaller store-room/office. Our purpose in life was to cover the electrical servicing of aircraft belonging to the Communications Flight. As previously mentioned, at Habbaniyah we had the Air Headquarters of Levant Command. The Communications Flight provided the transport for Command to visit outlying stations. Also previously mentioned was my inexperience of the electrical services of various aircraft, so, I was on a fairly steep learning curve to "get up to speed", so to speak. All went well and, following a routine inspection by the Officer in charge of the Supply Section, I was congratulated on the way my section's store was organised. I considered this a real compliment because, officially, my small section was not supposed to carry any spare parts. I pointed out to the Inspecting Officer that I thought we could improve our performance if we were allowed to carry minimal spares. He agreed and we carried on as before.

December came and Christmas celebrations were being discussed. My corporal, a Scot, was fortunate enough to have been allocated a Married Quarter. He and his wife decided to throw a party on New Year's Eve, to which all members of the Section, and several other friends, would be invited. It was a good party and lasted well into New Year's Day.

As the man in charge of the section, I took it upon myself to be at work at the normal time on that day. In fact, I was the only electrician present. The Air Officer Commanding Levant Command was ready to go on leave in his Official Aircraft but the engines could not be started and the trouble seemed to be electrical. Naturally, I was called upon to clear up the trouble and I did my best to look as if I knew what I was doing. With a few friendly clues from the Engine Fitter, it was decided that the trouble lay in a relay and a replacement was required. Whilst this was being sought in the Main Stores, the rest of my team turned up and we were able to get the AOC away on holiday.

Soon after the above incident, a re-organisation of the Technical Wing took place. I hasten to add this was not due to the delayed AOC. I was now transferred to another Electrical Section, away from the flying side of the unit. In effect, a new Maintenance Unit had been created and my new post was with that unit. I had a bigger Section employing six or seven airmen and an equal number of civilian electricians. Our job was to overhaul components from aircraft and ground equipment on the station. We were now dealing with aircraft, motor transport, airfield lighting and hospital equipment. This carried on until a second Electrical Officer arrived on the scene.

At this time we were still getting conscripted personnel known as National Serviceman. Every man over the age of 18 years was required to serve two years in one of the armed services. By signing on for the minimum contract of three years, these people could be classed as Regular Airmen and qualify for an enhanced rate of pay and somewhat better conditions of service. One of our officers had taken advantage of the longer service whilst the other decided that two years was enough. Now the powers-that-be decided that it was time for another reorganisation of the Electrical Section. The section was to be divided into an Air Electrical team and a Ground Electrical team with an officer in charge of each and a Senior NCO to be his deputy. One NCO was already on the scene, myself, an Air Electrician, a second Senior NCO appeared on the scene, a Ground Electrician. The new teams were announced with me in charge of the Ground team, with the new officer, whilst the existing officer and the new Ground Electrician took over the Air team.

I was responsible for three Corporals and half-a-dozen men, of which one corporal and two airmen were attached to the motor transport pool, three men were working in the Battery Charging Room on a shift basis and the other two Corporals and one airman were in the section with me.

Most of our work involved the airfield lighting system. Since the airfield was below the river level for most of the year, we had on-going problems with water seepage. Most of the taxi-ways and occasionally the runways were under water most of the time. For ease of access the blue lights marking the taxi-ways were on the surface rather than fixed in the ground. Each morning, the first job for one of the Corporals was to cycle round the airfield to check that the lights were working or needing attention. Nearly every day there would be two or three lights needing attention. Sometimes the trouble was water ingress causing short-circuit but on occasions we would find a broken cable and, alongside it, the body of a wild dog which had bitten the live cable, probably mistaking it for a snake, and been electrocuted. As the airfield was outside the perimeter fence, there was no way we could keep the dogs out. We were also responsible for servicing the Flasher Beacon, which flashes a recognition code for the benefit of passing aircraft.

On fairly rare occasions we might be called upon to service Hospital equipment. On one occasion we were informed that an Iron Lung, in use by a patient, was giving trouble, so I went with a corporal, who normally looked after hospital equipment. The patient was a female member of the Embassy staff from Baghdad, suffering from Poliomyelitis, and the machine was over-heating badly. We checked as best we could and decided the only solution was to change the drive motor.

We went, hot-foot, to Main Stores and, after much searching of handbooks, found the one spare motor available. This was no real surprise for, if a piece of equipment was likely to be used once in, perhaps, fifteen years, we could not expect to find half-a-dozen spares. Back to the hospital we went and prepared to make the change-over. Fortunately, the machine was fitted so it could be hand-operated and we shared the work. The old motor was removed and the new one fitted in its place.

However, after a comparatively short time it was apparent that the new motor, also, was over-heating. Our only solution was to turn to manual operation and take turns . This was tiring work and we had to keep going throughout that afternoon and all night. Next morning the Doctor came to check his patient who, unfortunately, had passed away. He congratulated us for our efforts and stressed that we did all we could. The girl was very ill and they had not expected her to recover.

There were at that time, I suppose, about fifty members of the Women's Royal Air Force at Habbaniyah. Their jobs were varied but mostly clerical or connected with a Signals Unit. They were treated well by most people but, for their own safety, were housed in a group of buildings surrounded be a tall fence topped with razor-wire. One of their buildings was used as a recreation room where they could hold dances every few weeks and, naturally, the girls could invite their male friends. On dance nights the room was decorated and my section had a standing order to provide coloured lights and a mirror-ball which rotated in front of spotlights. The installation of these lights would take us perhaps half a day and we would be invited to the dance as a reward. I was never a dancer, having two left feet, but would go along to the dances for a change of company.

The WRAF admin sergeant belonged to the same sergeants' mess as I did and, as she was due for repatriation in the near future, she asked me if I would like to take over one of her voluntary duties. Habbaniyah had its own recreational broadcasting station known as Forces Broadcasting Station, Habbaniyah. A Flight Lieutenant was in charge of the station with a sergeant, June Oliver, as his deputy and half-a-dozen boys and girls who gave up part of their spare time to man the station. The programme content was mainly recorded music interspersed with relayed BBC News bulletins. Reception of these bulletins was often very poor so the operators used their imagination to fill up a programme, either the operators' choice or requests from listeners. June had been in the post for some time and was keen that I would be her successor.

I went along and did an audition in front of several of the other announcers. My audition was pronounced successful and I started to find my way round the record library. I found the job interesting and tried to make my programmes as varied as I could with our fairly meagre resources. I have an interest in classical music and, occasionally tried to put on a concert. Nothing very lavish, but I would have an overture, perhaps a concerto followed by a symphony. I'm pleased to say I received some compliments from listeners.

We used to start the day with a Reveille program at about six a.m. This was literally, just a call up for heavy sleepers. On occasions when I did this programme, I started to introduce a recording of the Massed Bands of the Black Watch, or other pipe band. I must say I was surprised at the welcome comments I received. Most of the other members of my broadcasting staff were members of the Signals Unit and worked on a shift pattern. Naturally, RAF work took precedence over the radio station and, at times, it was difficult to find someone available for broadcasting duty. At these times I tended to fill the deficit myself and find I was doing far more shifts than I should. There was one other member of staff who could almost always, help me out. Mrs Peggy Bolt, the wife of a Group Captain in Air Headquarters, lived in Officers' Married Quarters, was very popular with our listeners and would often come in to help me out at very short notice.

I was coming near to the end of my contract with the RAF and, in my spare time, was trying to study, by correspondence course, to prepare myself for civilian life. My study was coming a very poor second to my other interests and I decided that I must give up broadcasting.

I had been on the waiting list for a married quarter ever since I arrived on the camp. There were only forty Airmen's Married quarters to satisfy the demands of the whole of Levant Command and the ruling was that it was uneconomical to bring an airman's family out from the UK if their stay would be for less than six months. I reached the top of the waiting list on the very day that I had six months left in Iraq, so I was told that I was not eligible for a married quarter as my family could not arrive in time to stay for six months. Within a few days I found myself being posted to Shaibah, on the Persian Gulf near Basra, to relieve the Sergeant who would take over "my" married quarter.

Shaibah was, to all intents and purposes, an insurance policy. It was on the route to several other stations in the Gulf area and further eastwards, and could be used as an alternative halt should an aircraft be in trouble or if weather or any other reason made it dangerous to continue a flight. In the four-and-a-half months that I was there, I only remember one aircraft landing there and that was a Canberra on a record attempt, with its own travelling crew.[1] I'm afraid that I succumbed to that infamous ailment 'The Shaibah Blues', a form of depressive illness which is best cured by a spell in bed with medical attention. In my case it lasted only about ten days but was very debilitating. I suspect it was brought on by the sheer boredom of the place.

My homeward trip from Shaibah took me back to Habbaniyah from where, for some obscure reason, several of us went by a small aircraft, by short stages, along the southern edge of the Mediterranean then Malta and Ystres, near Marseilles and finally to Lyneham in Wiltshire.

Shortly before I went to Iraq, Joan and I had moved into a brand new Council house in Romford, Essex. It was our first home outside the RAF and would, we thought, be our first home in civilian life. I had less than six months of my RAF service to serve and the time had come to sample "Civvy Street". Those last few months of service were to be spent at RAF Wittering, near Stamford in Lincolnshire where, I found,

---

[1] Editor's note: details of this record braking attempt are contained in another Woodfield book, *National Service Erk* by Ron Swain, one of the RAF mechanics aboard the Canberra aircraft in the London-Christchurch Air Race of 1953.

nobody really wanted me because I had such a short period to serve. I helped out where I could and made a few friends.

In March 1956 I went through the time-honoured process of clearance prior to discharge and then on four weeks leave, my final leave from the RAF ... or so I thought. During that leave I made strenuous efforts to find a job ready for the 1st April, my thirtieth birthday and my first day as a civilian. I found a job in a factory making paint. At my interview they explained that I would be trained in all aspects of paint making, almost like an apprenticeship, and, subject to my talents and wishes, could find myself in any of the departments of the company. I was quite happy and went home pleased with myself.

However, during the very last week of my leave, the RAF dropped a bombshell on my plans. The Government announced a new pay deal for the Forces which would increase my service pay by some ten shillings a week and would give to anyone who signed on for further service a tax free sum of £300. In today's financial world that sounds like peanuts but in 1956 it was a very good deal indeed. I could have bought a brand new car and several gallons of petrol for that much. After much discussion, Joan and I agreed that I should try to sign on for a further ten years. To cut the proverbial long story short, I was accepted and returned to Wittering, where I was to spend the next three-and-a half years.

22. Bomber Command Development Unit

At first I returned to the same Section I had recently left, the Aircraft Servicing Section, which was responsible for the electrical servicing of Canberras and Valiant Bombers, as part of their periodic servicing pattern.

I soon became reasonably acquainted with Canberras and enjoyed my work on them. The Valiant bombers were the first of the, so-called, 'V Bombers' to come into service and were quite new to me. The first of these aircraft was due to come into our hangar for its first Minor Servicing after about forty hours flying. The electrical rig for testing the aircraft's electric generators was giving trouble. The generators were capable of producing some 22½ kilowatts of electrical power and the test rig had been designed to test them to at least half of that capacity. Things kept going wrong and the rig would shut down prematurely. One day, I was asked to look over the set-up and try to suggest a solution. I noticed that the rig more or less duplicated the aircraft circuitry and asked if that was really necessary. When testing there was always at least one electrician watching to see how it performed. I thought that the aircraft circuitry needed to operate without supervision but the test rig was operating with a deal of supervision. After discussion with other technicians, I decided to reduce the Test Circuitry to a minimum and let the humans watch for problems. As the first aircraft for testing was now actually in the hangar, my solution was accepted. We simplified the test circuit and tested it.

Everything seemed to go according plan, the modification was accepted and the first Valiant Servicing was carried out.

Shortly after this episode, I was sent to work on 100 Squadron, Bomber Command Development Unit (BCDU) at the other end of Wittering's airfield, so I never knew whether the test rig modification was accepted by the authorities. My new squadron flew English Electric Canberras and carried out trials on new and existing bomber equipment. At the time, much of our work was highly classified but I believe the intervening time will have reduced that secrecy. My tour of duty at BCDU lasted from late 1956 to 1st February 1960, during which time we lived in Married Quarters in Wittering village. By this time our family had increased to two girls, Susan and Helen. The second of these, Helen, had arrived in August 1956, some eleven months after my return from Iraq and, incidentally, some six-and-a-half years after her sister. Both girls were very healthy and, fortunately, grew up that way. Apart from the usual children's maladies, they never caused us any worries.

Much of my time at BCDU was spent working on a Canberra B.I.8, which was, in layman's terms, a fighter/bomber version of this extremely versatile aircraft. In that time of nuclear threats we were adapting the Canberra to carry, and deliver, nuclear weapons. With conventional weapons these can be dropped, quite safely, whilst the delivery aircraft was reasonably close to the target. With a nuclear weapon the delivery must be as far away from the detonation as possible. If the aircraft flying on a straight course dropped a nuclear weapon and carried on flying in a straight line, he may well be directly above the target when the bomb exploded. This could be disastrous for aircraft and crew. By flying, at low altitude and steady speed, the pilot could, at a predetermined point, pull the aircraft up into a loop and the weapon would be automatically released at a certain point in the flight. The weapon would carry on the same course whilst the aircraft completed three quarters of a loop, giving maximum separation at the time of explosion. We tried this method of delivery and it was adopted by all types of bomber.

During this period there was a great deal for us technicians to worry about. There seemed to be a general trend towards reducing the size of the Armed Forces. We received frequent indications that most non-commissioned members of the RAF would not be able to serve beyond their fortieth birthday. Weighing up my qualifications and experience, I felt I might find it difficult to find employment in civilian life. The answer seemed to be, enrol with the local Technical College and earn some qualification which would be recognised by civilian employers. So, having gained permission from the RAF, I went along to Peterborough Technical College and registered for a course in Mechanical Engineering, my first love.

The RAF kindly allowed me to attend the college one day each week and I had to start studying seriously. Peterborough is about 11 miles from Wittering and I drove there with a friend who was studying Electrical Engineering. Most of the time it was a pleasant enough trip but, in the autumn and winter, the weather could provide serious problems. I recall one particular evening when the fog was really dense on the way home, so dense, in fact, that I could not see the side of the road on which we were travelling. The only way we could make even the slowest of progress was for Jack to sit on the left-hand wing of my old Rover car with a torch in his hand, giving me signals if I strayed too far from the kerb. We managed the journey without incident but very, very slowly.

23. Central Servicing Development Unit

Towards the end of 1959, I decided that, as I had been using Technical Publications for many years, it might be of interest, and use, to find out how they were produced. I therefore, applied to the Central Servicing Development Unit (CSDE), which, I found, was based at RAF Swanton Morley in Norfolk, and was responsible for all such publications.

After an interview with a Wing Commander at Swanton Morley, I was accepted and took up my new post on 1st February 1960. CSDE at that time consisted of a fair number of Technical Officers and a disproportionately large number of Technical Senior NCOs, who formed teams with specialist knowledge to consider all new aircraft, servicing equipment and procedures coming into, or proposed for, the Service. They would examine designs and discuss them with designers, make suggestions or modifications, as necessary, and devise Servicing Procedures for such equipment.

At first I was allocated to the Victor team, preparing Servicing Schedules for the new V-Bomber about to arrive in the service. After a few days, an Officer from CSDE met an Officer at BCDU in a conference at Wittering. I had done a considerable amount of work with the BCDU Officer and got on well. He apparently said to his colleague, "How is Sergeant Bartrop settling in to his new job?"

"I don't think I know that name," was the reply.

"You ought to get him on your team, he's good."

The BCDU man, Squadron Leader Freddie Cox, was one of the best men I have known, a true Officer and a Gentleman. Following their conversation, I was moved from the Victor team to the Armament Section of CSDE. I found the work very interesting as we made frequent visits, as a team, to manufacturers and Research Establishments. The only real problem with the job was that we might report for work on a Monday morning, only to be told to pack our bags because we were off to some far-flung station and would not be back until Friday afternoon. In short, the job was fine and interesting for the men, but hard for the wives and families, rather like a travelling salesman's job, I suppose.

In spite of the uncertainties of my job, I managed to keep up my studies at the Technical College, though now I had transferred to Norwich City College.

24. Education

In 1961, the dreaded National Service intakes ceased, with results that had not really been foreseen. The Technical Schools of the RAF relied on the services of young Graduates who would be enrolled as Education Officers. Drafted into the schools, these young chaps would teach the theoretical parts of the courses to trainee airmen. To cover the shortfall, the Air Ministry now called for Senior NCOs, with minimum qualifications of Ordinary National Certificate, to be seconded to the Education Branch for a period of two years. I thought I might like to be a teacher in Civvy Street, so I volunteered and was accepted. Along with twenty-four other like-minded chaps, I was posted to RAF Uxbridge, the RAF School of Education, for a three-month course in "How to teach".

Luckily, I took to the job like the proverbial fish to water and passed with flying colours and a very good grade. We were told at the start of the course that we would be given the opportunity to decide where we would like to be posted afterwards. As a former Engine Fitter, now Electrical Fitter, I said I would accept a posting to any Mechanical or Electrical School. Needless to say, I was posted to a Wireless and Radio School at Compton Bassett in Wiltshire!

No amount of protesting made any difference, so off I went, along with a friend, Norman, who felt as I did that we did not want to start learning about Radio Theory. We were both set to instruct on the first seven weeks of the training courses, which involved revising mathematics up to about "O" Level standard, and materials for conductors and insulators. We then went on to basic electrical theory, direct current theory and an introduction to alternating current theory. Norman was teaching telephonists whilst I had radio and radar mechanics. We both did quite well and obtained good results.

My fondness for playing soccer caused me to miss part of my allotted work when I suffered a Prolapsed Intervertebrate Disc (a slipped disc) in the first game of the season in August 1963. It was RAF policy that Wednesday afternoon was compulsory sports afternoon. This was a very painful experience that meant I must stay in hospital for two weeks, flat on my back, six weeks excused duty, six weeks half duty (mornings only and no prolonged standing) before I was allowed to resume normal duties. I was more than ready to resume my post before the end of that period but it gives a good impression of how the RAF cares for its staff when injured in the course of duty.

Towards the end of my secondment, the Senior Education Officer, a Wing Commander, called me to his office. I had no idea why such an exalted person should want to speak to me. Could I have inadvertently done something wrong? He asked me to sit down, congratulated me on the success of my period as an Education Officer and asked if I would consider applying to be commissioned and permanently seconded to the Education Branch. I was rather taken aback, as there had been no previous indication of any such suggestion. I thanked him very much for the honour he was proposing to do me but pointed out that in the seventeen years that Joan and I had been married, the RAF had been responsible for keeping us apart for more than six years. If I accepted his offer, I would have to spend several months on a Commissioning Course, probably on the Isle of Man, then go to University for at least a year to convert my

Higher National Certificate into a Degree. After all this, there could be no guarantee that we would be able to live together continuously for any length of time.

My wife was fed up with separation. I was fed up with separation and, thank you very much, but my marriage was more important to me than a Commission. I said it all very politely and, I must confess, I have had cause to question my decision from time to time. As an Education Officer, I could reasonably expect to reach the rank of Squadron Leader, with a far better salary than I had as a Chief Technician and a greatly enhanced pension at the end.

However, I did not accept the offer, which is probably just as well because when I told my wife of the offer she said, "If you want a Commission, go ahead, BUT I WILL NOT BE HERE!"

On completion of my two-year secondment I was sent back to Swanton Morley and CSDE, where I served the final part of my service career. Back in the same section of the Armament Squadron, I helped with the writing of Servicing Manuals once more and was soon promoted to be Editor of all papers produced in that section.

I tried to sound out the chances of a teaching post at the City Technical College but was told that I was not qualified to teach there, as my Service Career "was not equivalent to that expected of a teacher in an establishment preparing people for work in a factory situation". In other words, life and work in the Armed Forces was not commercial enough.

Nothing, it would seem, would change the situation. If I wanted to teach, it would have to be in a Secondary School and for that I would have to go to Teacher Training College and obtain a Teaching Certificate.

25. Return to Civilian Life

I applied to Norfolk Education Committee and was awarded a grant to cover my expenses whilst in college. The local Teacher Training College offered me a place and I began training as a teacher of Mathematics, with Science as a subsidiary subject. In view of my previous experience and qualifications, I was accepted for accelerated training, so I did only two years in college instead of three.

In the final two years of my engineering training, my course included quite a lot of calculus and, at last, I began to see why my early education in maths had been so boring. We were, of course, only learning the rules of maths. Only when one gets into more advanced, applied maths, do you realise how useful and interesting the subject can become.

In Teacher Training College I was given lots of past exam papers to practice and work through. I was happily spending my time working through the calculus questions when I discovered the syllabus had been changed. Now we should be learning Modern Mathematics rather than the Euclid and Pythagoras type. When I finally found myself in a classroom full of children and had to teach this so-called Modern Maths I began to wonder if, perhaps, I should have become an English teacher! Certainly, a degree in English might have made the language of the maths book more intelligible. Somehow I struggled through, although I was rarely completely at ease.

All schools are different and, as I had entered the profession late in life, I felt I could more quickly build up experience if I could work in a number of different schools. To this end, I changed school after, at most, two years. This seemed to work out all right but I began to feel it rather stressful. Each new school had its character and its characters, and they all had to be learned very quickly. Coupled with this, my old back injury started to give me trouble. The constant bending over desks was not the best position for a suspect spinal injury. I began to need to take time off school to repair my back. There were members of staff, some of them alleged friends, who thought I was 'swinging the lead' and having unnecessary time away. I can honestly say that never, in all my time in school, did I stay at home when I was fit for work. Eventually I felt I had to leave teaching and find other work.

I found employment with a firm of International Insurance Brokers in Norwich. The qualification for the job required two subjects at "A" level and the position was described as 'Insurance Technical Clerk'. Brokers, based in London, would go to see Members of Lloyds and coerce them into accepting part responsibility for an Insurance policy with values of, probably, millions of pounds, or dollars. The Members might take up five, ten or maybe fifteen per cent of the value. Some of the larger shares might be re-insured, that is, the member might ask a fellow insurer to cover part of the risk. When the broker had convinced enough people to cover the total amount at risk, he would send the list to me and I would adjust amounts to cover one hundred per cent of the risk. This might involve increasing some shares and reducing others. It may sound complicated and sometimes was, especially if there was much re-insurance on the list. Claims might follow and these had to be shared amongst all the members listed for that case.

My particular share of the market was with clients in many different countries. I had clients in America, Australia, South Africa and many others and involved all kinds of insurance. At one time I might be handling a policy for a race horse in America owned by a famous film star and next insurance for 500 laboratory rats being moved from one laboratory to another. Some of my policies were for people such as a famous orchestral conductor travelling to Australia. There was quite a variety.

One case which I inherited from the previous occupant of my desk concerned a man in America who, whilst working in a multi-storey building, decided to clean up his area. Finding a large sheet of plywood, he picked up one side of it and began to slide it across the floor. He moved it several feet, pushing it in front of him, until he disappeared through a hole in the floor that it had been concealing. He came to rest on the lower floor some twenty feet below. This had all taken place about ten years before I took on the job. I only found the full story when I suggested that, instead of paying the man annual payments, it would be cheaper if he could be persuaded to accept a lump sum. I learned that a settlement had been offered some time previously but had been ruled out. He had been badly injured and was still in a bad condition.

As I have said, I enjoyed the job and found it very interesting, but the pay was only about one third of what I could get teaching. When I discovered that I was being paid a reduced amount because they were taking into account that I was receiving a RAF pension, I started to look for another teaching post. I was, in fact, only receiving a part-pension from the RAF at that time, about £5 per month.

After three years in insurance I took the first teaching post I was offered. I was in the post for almost six years whilst my back caused me to have more and more time off. My absences caused much trouble for the school because they had to keep finding someone to stand in for me. There was, also, the damage to the children's education caused by the disruption. One day, I spoke to the Headmaster about the possibility of early retirement. He was agreeable and took the matter up with the authorities, who agreed that I should leave at the end of that school year. So I retired, at the age of 58 years, at the end of August 1982.

My wife Joan was still working full-time in an Insurance Office and was finding her job more and more stressful but she agreed to carry on for a couple of years so that we did not suffer a double reduction in our joint income. I still suffered many problems with my back and found my only relief from pain was to lie flat on my back on the floor for an hour or two at a time. Fortunately, both our girls were, by this time, married and living in their own houses, so I had only myself to worry about. I still spent a lot of time on my back but, on the better days, I did a little housework, and, by stages, prepared a meal for Joan and me when she came home from work.

After a time, when my back allowed, I might venture out into the city to do a little urgent shopping. After I had been retired for about six months, I received a letter, from the Ministry of Health, informing me that my Invalidity Benefit was to be reviewed. This came as a shock for I had never been told that there was a possibility of it being reduced. I was required to present myself for a medical examination by a Ministry doctor. The examination took place in an office on the top floor of a three-storey office building in the centre of Norwich. On arrival I found that the lift was Out of Order so I would have to climb the stairs. This was, fairly obviously, a part of the examination.

Without any play-acting, it took a long time for me to climb those stairs.

I found that the people carrying out these examinations were retired doctors who were paid a set fee for their time. The test itself was a farce, consisting of many questions and simple physical tests like leaning forward until it hurt or turning this way or that. At the end of my "examination" it was decided that I was fit to work so long as it did not involve sitting, standing or walking for more than a few minutes at a time. Furthermore, I could not be expected to carry any weights. In fact, it seemed that if I got out of bed I would be in danger of exceeding my parameters. This procedure was repeated at intervals as I appealed against the findings. Eventually, I had to face a Tribunal consisting of a Chairman and two other members who, I was assured, were completely neutral.

After much discussion of the facts, I suggested that if I was fit enough to work, why could I not go back to teaching, not exactly a physically demanding profession. The Tribunal seemed to agree and decided that I was unfit for work. Whilst all of this had been going on my Invalidity Benefit had been discontinued and I was receiving Unemployment Benefit, at a much lower rate. When the position was finally settled I received a nice cheque for over four thousand pounds in back payments.

26. Living in France

After Joan retired, in 1984, we decided to change our lives completely and go to live in France. We had been to Provence for holidays several times since 1976 and loved the region, the people and, most of all, the way of life. Everything in France seemed to proceed at a much slower pace than in England. Besides, you could rely on the weather to be sunny, if, at times, a little too hot. After six or seven visits, we felt certain enough to invest in a mobile home on a permanent site in the Var. We had been introduced to a Domaine near the small town of Le Muy, about fifteen miles inland from the Mediterranean coast, at St Aygulf, and that is where we decided to settle.

The Domaine – in England it would probably be called an Estate – covered about 900 acres, spread over five hills, the highest being Le Peynier at almost 1,000 feet. The land had originally been the property of the Duchess of Le Muy, who gave it to a Canadian Army Officer as a reward for his help to the French Resistance Movement during World War II. He had been serving in the region at the time of the German Occupation and, after being evacuated to North Africa when the Allies left France, he had begged the Canadian authorities to allow him to return to France to help the Resistance Movement in Marseilles. Being a Signals Officer made him a very attractive proposition to the French and his Canadian bosses let him go. He stayed there until the war was over and was a major help to the French, and, no doubt, to the Allies with whom he doubtless communicated.

The Domaine, as I have said, was a gift from a very grateful lady and the new owner, at first, was at a loss to know what to do with it. Travelling home to Canada one day he saw a site devoted to Camping and Caravanning and had the idea to set up a similar project at Canebières. The name, incidentally, comes from the Headquarters of the Resistance Movement, in that part of France, which was situated in the Rue de Canebières. (Strangely, Canebières is the French name for the bush which produces Cannabis, though no such bush has ever been found on the Domaine).

Captain Brown, for such was the Canadian's name, was a man of very fixed ideas. His holiday Domaine was to be open to all nationalities except Germans. He would not entertain the idea of allowing a German so much as a view of the Domaine. He brought a bulldozer on to the site and, little by little, cut roads across the hillsides and, from the roads, cut terraces of various sizes on which people would make their homes. Each plot was numbered and served with mains water, electricity and drains, and was advertised in many national daily papers. At first there were mainly tents and touring caravans but, gradually, more and more people brought mobile homes onto the site. The whole set-up was organised and supervised by Captain Brown. He was determined that Canebières should be a respectable place where people could enjoy their freedom without interference from anyone. He would patrol the place looking for signs of trouble, friction, call it what you will, and woe betide any occupant who left washing on the line beyond lunch-time or let his dog cause trouble for the neighbours. The first malpractice would bring a warning but repetition would bring more positive measures. Brown carried a revolver at all times and would not hesitate to shoot a badly behaved dog.

As the site was developed, roads were surfaced and street lighting installed, there was an armed guard on duty in the guardroom at the gate twenty-four hours a day and 365 days per year. Entry was limited to owners of plots and guests they had invited, for whom they were responsible. Rubbish was to be taken to large skips near the entrance to the Domaine and these skips were regularly emptied.

The Domaine was regulated by a Committee of elected owners and everything went very smoothly. Eventually, there were 771 registered plots on the Domaine, most of which, about 500, were occupied by French owners, with a good sprinkling of British families, about 100, with Italians in the remainder. From time to time there were other nationalities present, including one Australian lady, who had actually bought a Land Rover so she could drive overland (with necessary ferry connections of course) all the way from Perth in Australia to France. She was a veritable Free Spirit and seemed to enjoy roughing it. On her last visit, she celebrated her 83rd birthday.

The plots, as I have indicated, were of varying sizes, though few overlooked each other. My own plot was on a steep part of the Domaine and covered 639 square metres. Originally, it was equipped with an old British Mobile Home which had two bedrooms, bathroom, kitchen-diner and toilet and, believe it or not, gas-fired central heating. We spent many happy holidays in her but eventually the time came for a change. We bought a new home from a French firm and looked on in awe as they removed the old home and replaced it with the new model. Because of the steepness of the terrain and the narrowness of the roads, the process took all day. This new home was slightly smaller than the original but much more comfortable. After a year or two, we decided to add an extension beside the unit which doubled the habitable area. This, in itself, was a mammoth task, for Joan and I did all the work ourselves. Overall, it took us nearly three years to complete and we lived in it all the time. The addition consisted of two rooms, one a double bedroom and the other became our sitting room. The original single bedroom became a utility room with plenty of store cupboards and worktops. The original kitchen/diner was somewhat enlarged. Outside, we had been obliged to make the plot wider, which involved building a retaining wall to prop up the mountainside. The new development incorporated a small, covered patio for outside dining. We already had a large patio for barbecues and the like, an outside *cabine sanitaire* with toilet, shower/ washing room with mains water and sanitation. We had never gone in for DIY on such a scale so we were very pleased with ourselves and the results. I am very pleased to report that, after nearly twenty years, everything is still in working order and the retaining wall still retains.

Incidentally, the Domaine is still as popular as ever but the mobile homes are giving way to villas and almost every plot which has spare space now has a miniature swimming pool where the occupants can cool off in hot weather. We sold our interest in the place in 2000, as we were then both well into our seventies and it was becoming too much to drive down there and spend the first two weeks clearing the weeds before we could start to enjoy a rest.

The Domaine Des Canebières is now, definitely, an up-market place for the well-to-do to spend their time. It is definitely out of our reach and we are glad we left when we did.

27. My Parents

Meanwhile, on the home front in England, things were changing, inexorably. My father died in 1977, after a long illness and dementia. Mum had nursed him through all of this – with precious little help from the authorities. I was living and working in Norwich at the time and had written to the Medical Officer of Health in Sheffield, asking that my father be taken into hospital in order to protect my mother's health. I received no answer and no action was taken by the authorities. Within 24 hours of my father's death, Mum was rushed to hospital following a massive haemorrhage. Nobody realised how ill she had become whilst nursing her sick husband. She spent seventeen weeks in hospital and had three major abdominal operations in that time. I made twenty trips to Sheffield in that time, to see her and, on several occasions Joan and I would take her out of the hospital and into Derbyshire, always a favourite place for our family. At first she did not know she had been out, but, gradually, her condition improved and she began to recognise places and her condition improved. Several times, on my return to my home, I received phone calls from the hospital, to the effect that, if I wanted to see her alive I had better come immediately. Most of the time she had very little idea who I was and was becoming severely institutionalised. She was hallucinating and, on occasion, would accuse her Irish nurse of being a member of the IRA, and would attempt to strike her.

When Mum came out of hospital, my brother Dennis took it upon himself to visit her, in her home, every day. He lived in

Sheffield so he was slightly more available than me but he had a business to run and it must have increased his workload considerably. She made reasonable progress but she was never the old Mum we knew and loved, Surprisingly, she hung on to life for eleven years after Dad died and finally passed away at breakfast time on 20th January, exactly as her husband had done.

28. Joan's Parents

Joan's mother died, very suddenly, in 1975. It was a Saturday evening and she and her husband were watching television, one of those game shows, I believe. At the interval she stood up to make a cup of tea and fell dead at her husband's feet. He was distraught and tried to give her the kiss of life, as best he could, but to no avail. When the doctor came he said she had died of a massive heart attack and, even if he had been in the room, nothing could have saved her. Joan's father, Fred, came to live with us after that and slowly began to get over his loss, though, on one occasion he walked out and made his way to the Garden of Rest where she was interred.

Eventually, he decided that he would like to go into a retirement home. We could not deter him from this and he went to a Local Authority home in Aylsham, where he had his own room with television and his own radio. I doubt whether he really enjoyed being there. He was a Big City man and they were Country Bumpkins. He was not stuck up or stand-offish in any way but he did not understand them and they never understood him; a real oil and water situation.

One morning a nurse was making her rounds to see that everyone was getting ready for breakfast. As she approached his door, she could hear his electric razor, whirring away. 'No need to worry about Fred,' she thought, and carried on with her round. He did not appear for breakfast and they found him, dead, in his chair, razor still in his hand.

It was April 1982 and he was 94 years old.

Fred Fleming had never had an easy life. His father had been a ship's engineer, one of the first in the early days of steam ships. His father was a Scottish Presbyterian Minister, a very strict man who would never brook the slightest deviation from his regime. On one of his home-leaves, the sailor made the mistake of having, in his possession, a bottle of whisky. The minister was furious and turned his son, together with his newly pregnant wife, out onto the street. Fortunately, they were able to find lodgings and soon settled in.

But troubles seldom come singly and on his next voyage the sailor was killed in an accident on board ship. His distraught widow decided to leave Scotland and, with her female companion, went to live in London. On 7th September 1887, Fred made his appearance, a healthy eight-and-a-half pound baby. He had a reasonably normal childhood in the female-dominated household, did quite well at school and, as a teenager, loved to play football on the nearby Lea Marshes with his friends.

An elevated railway line, supported on a series of arches, crossed the marshes and several of the arches were rented by various individuals where they stored things, made furniture in small workshops, or carried out other activities. Fred was particularly intrigued by the efforts of two men who had a workshop in one of the arches. In the very earliest days of the 20th Century, they were trying to build and fly an aeroplane! Time and again they would wheel their craft out on to the field, start its engine and taxi it around. Fred was fascinated, having just started an engineering apprenticeship, and wondered who the men could be. Sadly, he never found out. Many years later, when reminiscing about his early years, he would tell the story of these two men and wonder who they could have been. By pure chance, I found out, sadly after Fred's death, that one of those men was almost certainly Alliott Verdon-Roe,[2] who went on to become the founder of Avro, the aircraft manufacturers who produced the Lancaster bomber, which played such a critical role in World War II.

But, I digress... Fred completed his apprenticeship but had trouble finding employment. This problem was solved by the onset of World War I. Fred volunteered and was accepted in the Royal Horse Artillery, where he served throughout the war achieving the rank of sergeant. After the war was over, he again found it impossible to find employment. The end of hostilities signalled a period of depression with high unemployment figures, particularly in engineering. After a frustrating time he decided to try the woodworking industry and, eventually found his place in a firm in Bethnal Green. He stayed with that firm for 43 years, all through World War II and up to his retirement at the age of seventy years.

Fred's wife, Lizzie, was an orphan, the daughter of an alcoholic mother and an absentee father. She had a fairly hard upbringing in an orphanage and, as soon as she was old enough, was put into service as a housemaid with a Jewish family. In this she was lucky, for the family for whom she worked treated her very well indeed. She met Fred when he was sent by his employer to do some work in her employer's house. Their relationship

---

[2] Sir Alliott Verdon-Roe OBE, Hon. FRAeS, FIAS (1877-1958) was born in Manchester and was the first Englishman to fly an all-British machine at Lea Marshes on 12th July 1909.

He founded AV Roe and Co in Manchester with his brother Humphrey on 1st January 1910. A.V. Roe and Co became one of the most successful British aviation companies, building iconic aircraft bearing the Avro marque, such as the 504, Tutor, Anson, Lancaster, Lancastrian, York, Shackleton and Vulcan.

Alliott left AV Roe and Co in 1926 and in 1928 was knighted and established Saunders-Roe, builders of flying boats based at Cowes on the Isle of Wight; he remained Chairman of this company until his death in 1958.

progressed and they soon realised they were in love and decided to marry in 1919. Their first child was born the following year and three more children arrived at, roughly, two year intervals.

In the early 1930s, with their growing family of three girls and a boy, life in their small flat in a crumbling slum in Stepney was becoming very crowded. At any one time, one or other of the children would be ill. The youngest, Joan, fared the worst. Almost from birth she had been a sickly child and this culminated in a serious chest ailment at the age of two years. For a long time she was desperately ill and not expected to survive. The Flemings were not a religious family, indeed Fred had some very scathing criticisms of The Church in later years, but it was thanks to the Salvation Army that Joan eventually pulled through. I do not know how the Army came to hear of her illness but they made arrangements for her to be admitted to Hackney Hospital where she could have the vitally necessary surgical treatment. The operation was a complete success and the girl, at last began to grow stronger. But her troubles were far from over. An epidemic of measles hit the hospital and, of course Joan had to have her share of spots.

The hospital's doctors had strongly recommended a move to the country. Indeed, some of them had said it was vital if Joan was to make any sort of progress. Doctors are always very good at recommending ideal courses of action, but what was Fred to do? He had no financial reserves he could plunder. He was a journeyman carpenter/joiner with a wife and four children to feed and house. For a time he despaired of ever being in a position to move anywhere, let alone into the country. He was, however, a resourceful man possessed of infinite patience and an indomitable spirit. If the children needed to move to the country, then move they would. Week by week he schemed and planned. Copper by copper his "country" fund grew. Each night, when his work-mates went home, and every weekend, he spent making furniture for the new home he had yet to find. Somehow, he also made time to go out into the country looking at new houses. Lizzie and he finally found something they thought they could manage to live in. They found a three-bedroom terrace house, with a decent garden, not too far from the shops and public transport. Beyond the end of the garden, nearly fifty yards long, were fields as far as the eye could see, running down to and beyond, the River Rom. All Fred needed now was a deposit of twenty-five pounds and three pounds eighteen shillings (£3.90) per month for the next twenty-five years.

All that summer the children played in the fields and along the riverbank. After the polluted air and confined spaces, this country atmosphere gave them a new lease of life and they all grew stronger and healthier. Even young Joan, the baby of the family, began to grow stronger. Most of her earlier years had been spent in hospitals but now that was all behind her. She began to fill out and was soon out-running, out-jumping and out-fighting her newly found playmates. The change in her was nothing short of miraculous.

Of course, the new life was not without its drawbacks, though these were not too onerous. Any spare time that Fred had now was spent in the garden. He took great pride in his plot and soon had it all planned. For half its length he laid out a lawn surrounded by a narrow concrete path, which he laid himself, flanked by flowerbeds. The boundary of this section was marked with a rustic fence with an archway in the middle. He planned for this to have rambling roses and honeysuckle growing over the arch and built in two seats so that Lizzie and he could take advantage of the long summer evenings. Beyond the arch was to be the kitchen garden, where he would grow potatoes, vegetables and perhaps a few loganberry, gooseberry and currant bushes. He might even get a few chickens later on. They would provide fresh eggs in exchange for the kitchen scraps that would otherwise be wasted.

Perhaps the biggest problem in their new life was the distance from Fred's work. He was still employed as a carpenter in Bethnal Green where he was held in high regard by his firm. Employment was not so plentiful that a man could give up a good, secure post just because of a small matter of travelling 12 miles. At first, Fred would walk the two miles to Romford Station, then catch the train to Liverpool Street Station. But times were hard and he could hardly afford the train fare. To Fred's way of thinking there was only one solution; he would have to buy a bicycle.

"After all," he reasoned, "what is twelve miles to a man like me? I'm not an old man, not even fifty yet." So he bought his bicycle and every day, in all weathers, he cycled the twelve miles to Bethnal Green. Along the Eastern Avenue he went, all through the Second World War, until he was well into his sixties. He quite enjoyed the ride, most days, and soon made a friend of a younger man who lived and worked near him.

One day, Fred was unwell and stayed at home. His young friend cycled alone. As he rode past a parked car, the driver opened his door and knocked the cyclist off his cycle and under the wheels of a passing lorry. The young man was killed outright, leaving a widow and two young children. Fred, on hearing of this terrible accident a few days later, vowed he would never ride to work again and consequently resumed his journey by bus and train until the end of his working life.

By this time, Romford had changed considerably. No longer did Fred's back garden look out over fields. Everywhere houses had been built, part of a huge development that had consumed almost every scrap of available land. The town had spread itself like an enormous ink-blot, enveloping everything in sight. Once again Fred's thoughts turned to a home in the country, just a little cottage for "me and the old woman", as he affectionately called her. But he felt he still had responsibilities to his family. True, the eldest girl, Doris, was married and had started a family and Freddie, the son, was making a career for himself in the Army. Second daughter, Lily, was working in London and had a flat near to her place of work, whilst the younger sister and I planned to be married at Christmas. That left just young Pat, the baby of the family. Born in Romford, Pat was near to her nineteenth birthday and was serving a short engagement in the WRAF. As Fred saw things, his duty was to provide a home for her until she decided to leave home permanently or until she married.

"It would not be fair," he reasoned, "to bury her in the depths of the country. Might spoil her chances of a good marriage."

Fred left his carpenter's job just after his seventieth birthday, having worked the extra years to improve his retirement pension (by just one pound per week) and now he felt he deserved a rest. Over the last few months he had been casting an eye over the property market. All he needed was a cottage – two up and two down would do – with a nice bit of garden to keep him occupied. At last, he found what he wanted. It was, in fact, a pair of cottages with vacant possession of one. Both had electricity but he would have to get mains water connected. Main drains would have to wait a while – still, chemical toilets were acceptable and washing water could be thrown on the garden.

The cottages were in the tiny rural village of Stockton, Norfolk, about three miles from Beccles on the Suffolk border.

It was just about this time that Pat announced her engagement. She had met a young Irishman in the RAF and they were to be married within a year, when they were both due to complete their military service. Fred could see the end of his responsibilities and decided to go ahead with his move.

He sold the Romford house to his son, Freddie; that way they both got a good deal, he felt, the young man got a house and his father could get a quick sale and was able to buy his dream house. The removal was completed without too much trouble and the Flemings began to settle in their new surroundings. Everything seemed to be going according to plan, then, Pat's engagement was broken. When she left the RAF she came to live wither parents in Trevora Cottage. Fortunately there was plenty of room for her and she soon found employment in Beccles. Within a year, she had met a local boy, son of a farm manager, and they married and settled down in their own house in Beccles.

Trevora Cottage was one of a semi-detached pair, built around 1800 and surrounded by almost an acre of land. The original building was, typically of its period, of Norfolk red bricks with a pan-tile roof. The ground floor of each cottage consisted of a living room, perhaps fourteen feet square, and a small kitchen-cum-dining room, perhaps ten feet by six feet wide. The remaining plan was completed by a walk-in pantry. In the early part of the twentieth century, both cottages had been enlarged by the addition of lean-to extensions to provide a bathroom with toilet, but neither had the luxury of piped water. That had to be carried in buckets from the well across the lane – Well Lane- on which they stood. The upper floor of each cottage was reached by a very narrow, steep, winding staircase and consisted of two bedrooms. Each cottage also boasted a small porch which helped, considerably, to reduce the draughts which permeated the gaps around the front doors.

After eight years in this cottage Lizzie and Fred had never regretted their move. They had settled into country life as comfortably as if they had been born to it. Their cottage had been modernised and now had hot and cold water, flush toilet and a bathroom. They were even connected to the mains. In short, they were happy in their new home and had never considered leaving it. But Fred was now seventy-nine! It is true, he could still cycle the mile-and-a-half to the Post Office for their "wages" every Thursday, and he frequently cycled the three miles to Beccles for some urgent shopping. On summer afternoons he would cycle round the country lanes and had even ventured into Lowestoft, some twelve miles away. But, suppose something should happen to him, he wondered. Lizzie couldn't get around much these days. Stockton had no shop, no bus service and was a pretty isolated place to be in.

On her twenty-first birthday, Lizzie had stumbled on some stairs and, as she learned many years later, had cracked her pelvis. Forty-five years after the fall, which had often caused her pain which she had borne in silence, she was thoroughly examined. "There is a crack in your pelvis", the doctor told her."It is getting wider and is in danger of splitting your pelvis across to the hip-socket". The doctor persuaded her to have an operation to insert a pin which would draw the crack together. At the same time, the doctor said, he could lengthen her left leg which was some three inches shorter than the right one. After a total of six months in hospital, mostly in a plaster cast, stretching from waist to ankle, she finally returned home to convalesce and was bitterly disappointed to find that her lengthened leg was now too long! Despite the hospitals reassurances that they could correct it, she decided not to have a second operation and learned to manage, as before, on her odd legs.

Lizzie was happy enough pottering about the house or, in summer, sitting in the garden with a good book. She could not walk far, at first, but that did not matter. Fred could get around on his bicycle. She was content.

October was almost passed and the few leaves remaining on the trees were a rich golden brown in the weak rays of the sun. There was a nip in the air, which made winter seem even closer, and the old man rubbed his hands briskly together as he straightened up from his digging. Throughout the year, he had lavished his tender care on that patch of earth, watching the fruits of his efforts as they approached maturity, and now he was reaping his harvest. Each turn of the fork uncovered plump, clean potatoes and, beside him on the path were boxes and bags of carrots, Swedes and turnips. It had been a good year and the old man's heart sang within his breast.

But, Fred was now seventy-nine and, as he eased his back from the digging this afternoon, he felt every day of it. "It's no good", he muttered to the blackbird which always followed him around the garden, darting in to take advantage of the worms and leather-jackets turned up by Fred's fork. "I can't be bothered with this garden any more. It's not that I can't do it. I can't be bothered". The bird cocked his head and looked at Fred, appearing to understand every word. Perhaps he did for Fred would often pass the time of day with his feathered friends, usually the blackbird and a perky robin, who also stole an occasional worm.

Nobody, seeing Fred for the first time, would have guessed his age. A little below average height, his stocky figure belied his nearly four-score years. True, his hair was white and thinning but his shoulders were broad and his back straight and there was a spring in his step, except on damp days when he might limp a little from a war-wound picked up in the Battle of the Somme in World War I.

As he meticulously cleaned the mud from his boots and fork and put them away in the shed for another day, his mind was in turmoil. Where could he find a small house, nearer the shops, with less garden to tire him? Who would want to buy this cottage? The adjoining cottage, next door, was let, at a very nominal rent, to another old couple, even older than Fred and Lizzie. He couldn't just turn them out. His conscience would never allow him to do such a thing.

A few days later, Joan and I came to visit the old couple. We lived in Norwich, only about twenty miles away and liked to keep an eye on the old ones. During the evening the subject came up in conversation.

"How can I move?" the old man asked. "I've got no money and no chance to raise any."

"But, Dad," said I, "You've got these two cottages. They will fetch a decent price and you can use that to buy somewhere else. Let me have a look round for you and I'll let you know what I find."

My first call was in the nearby town of Loddon which, though it did not boast an Estate Agency, it had a Solicitor.

"Sorry to bother you," said I, as I was shown into an office that was obviously used for work rather than for show. I explained my father-in-law's situation to the solicitor, who smiled and asked, "What made you come to my office?"

"Because there is no Estate Agency and I thought, you were the next best thing," I said with a smile.

"You must be psychic," said the solicitor. "As a matter of fact I have a client who has a terraced house for sale, right here in the main street. It may well be satisfactory for your in-laws."

Arrangements were made for the old folk to view the property and they loved it at first sight. Within a few days the vendor had agreed to take the pair of cottages in exchange for the house near the centre of Loddon. Fred's neighbours were able to arrange accommodation with their son and the move was completed in record time.

Fred and Lizzie were delighted with their new home, which was more roomy and modernised than their cottage. Lizzie was now able to walk to the shops for the first time in many years. Fred could walk to the Post Office for their pensions instead of having to cycle. At the end of their garden, a gate opened on to the quayside and the River Chet. Here, the old couple could watch the holidaymakers on their Broads Cruisers, or marvel at the variety of water birds which inhabited the area.

The Flemings enjoyed their new life for more than six years, until one fateful day, just before Christmas 1975, when Lizzie collapsed and died.

After the funeral, Fred could not face the prospect of staying in that house alone. Fortunately, he was able to come to live with us. His bedroom was at the rear of our house and looked out over farmland and sports fields. He would stand, for long periods, watching the various activities, harvest gathering or schoolboys' football matches. Sometimes, he would take our dog for a walk. Rex was a well-behaved German Shepherd and came to love and respect the old man.

Helen, the younger of our two daughters, was just finishing a three year tour of duty in the Army. She had become used to her independence and did not want to return to living in our house. With a little help from us, she was able to buy the cottage from her grandfather (needless to say, at a very reasonable price).

Fred, looking back over his life, felt he had completed a circle. His earliest years had been lived at the edge of a city and now, here he was at the edge of another city. What could the future hold for him?

We were still working full-time at this stage, so Fred was left alone for long periods. This did not worry him unduly; he had his meals, plenty of books to read and could always take the dog for a walk if he wished. In short, he was content. Or was he? He still spent a considerable amount of time looking out of that window. He enjoyed watching the youngsters playing football. As winter approached once more, we put a small electric fire in his bedroom to be sure he did not suffer from the cold. Fred was grateful and made sure he was not extravagant in the use of the fire. It was positioned under the window, just where he liked to stand. One day, Joan came home from work to find an awful smell in the house. Fred had stood too near the fire and had scorched his trousers. He was lucky because they were made of synthetic fibres, which did not burn. They could, so easily, have caught fire and perhaps set the house on fire.

We had a family conference to try to decide how a recurrence could be avoided without leaving Fred in the cold and Fred told me that he would like to move into a care home. The discussion became a little heated at times but the old man was adamant. We needed to work, he could not be left alone, so, he insisted, there was no other solution. The Local Council had a home at Aylsham, a few miles up the road, and was very helpful. We all made several visits to the home and Fred said he would like to move in when there was a vacancy.

The move was made one weekend and Fred settled in quite well but did not make many friends there. The other residents were far too countrified for a Big City boy like him. He was not an unfriendly man but to him they seemed to be waiting for the hearse whilst he felt he was waiting for a bus and still had a life to live.

One day, we were phoned by the Manageress of the home, who told us that Fred had passed away. Arrangements were made for a funeral and, eventually, Fred's ashes were scattered in the Garden of Rest at St. Faiths, with those of his beloved wife Lizzie.

29. Extended Families

I retired from my teaching post a few months after Fred's death and Joan retired two years later. We were living, at that time, in a detached house on the northern fringes of Norwich. Because of my state of health we decided to give up the house with its garden because I just could not cope with it as I would have liked. We did not rush into a sale. We decided we would like to have a flat either in the country or somewhere on the coast. Strangely, there do not seem to be many flats in the countryside so we settled on one on the sea-front at Cromer, on the north Norfolk coast. I believe the building had, at some time, been a small hotel but was converted into six self-contained flats. Each had three large bedrooms, separate bathroom and shower-room with toilet, a large kitchen and a large sitting-room cum dining room with two large bay windows looking out to the sea. An elderly couple, older than us, were living in the flat and, although they wanted to sell the flat, they did not want to move out until after Christmas 1985. The time was about the middle of November and the whole chain of buyers and sellers was geared up to settle right away. Rather than break the chain we put all our furniture into storage and went to stay with our daughter Helen, and her soldier husband in their Army married quarter in Germany. Fortunately their house was quite large enough for all of us, and their two young daughters. Everything went well until early January when I developed Gastritis, a very painful stomach condition. Frank managed to get me an appointment with the Garrison Medical Officer who prescribed something which, in the end, did not help very much. We found that the elderly couple were ready to leave the flat, so we decided to come home. The weather was quite bad, at that time, with temperatures, in Germany, down to minus 16 degrees Centigrade. The German authorities were well prepared and all main roads had been treated, so the drive across Germany to the ferry was reasonably easy. We boarded a ferry for Felixstowe, in Suffolk, and, when we left the town to take the road to Norwich we found that the roads, everywhere, were buried under snow up to 12 inches deep. There was very little we could do about it except to take to the road as carefully as possible. In the whole of that forty mile drive we saw only three other vehicles and I was able to keep up a reasonable speed.

Arriving in Norwich, our first task was to find somewhere to spend a couple of nights. We found a small 'hotel' near the railway station where we passed two fairly cheap, and not very cheerful, nights. I managed to contact a doctor who I knew and made an appointment. He soon decided I had contracted some other infection as well as Gastritis. No wonder the Army doctor's treatment had not been successful. I was soon on the road to recovery and we made arrangements for our furniture to be delivered and moved into our new home.

We decide that the kitchen would never be adequate for our needs. It was large enough but the previous occupants had managed with an ancient gas oven and one small cupboard. So, my first job was to design and install a new kitchen with modern cooker, washing-machine, fridge and lots of cupboards and work-tops. The fitting took a week or two and, meanwhile, we took our main meal in one of the local hostelries. It was hard work but it was worth the effort.

We managed to make the flat fairly comfortable and felt we had made a good move. Unfortunately we found the building had a cellar which had openings looking out to sea. These were protected by a grill which would prevent any person getting access to the basement from that side of the building. Most unfortunately, rats are not excluded by railings and they found their way into the building. I took the matter up with the "Letting Agent" who paid lip service to a cure but did not do very much to help. After further representations, I had a full survey carried out which discovered a number of serious deficiencies in the property. It was obvious that the whole building was in desperate need of lots of loving care. We were fortunate in that we still had our bolt-hole in France and spent a lot of time there. We owned that flat for several years and, when Frank finally left the Army, in 1993, he and his family came to live with us. By this time they had their full quota of two girls and a boy so the large bedrooms were very useful.

Joan and I continued to make frequent trips to France, leaving the family a bit more breathing space. Frank had a great deal of difficulty finding employment in civilian life. After spending twenty-four years in uniform and becoming the youngest Warrant Officer First Class in the Royal Signals Regiment, it seemed he was unemployable. In his first year out of the Army, he wrote 150 job applications without success. He only received about three answers to his letters. Finally, one day when he was making a visit to the Job Centre, Joan took a phone-call from someone who had known Frank in the Army. He asked that Frank should call a certain number where there was a vacancy which he might fill. He was successful and enjoyed the work for some time. They say all good things come to an end. In the IT business, where he was employed, there was a great crash, in the nineties. He was out of work again, along with many others.

When the Second Iraq War ended, Frank heard there were jobs available in Baghdad. He applied, was successful and worked in Baghdad for an American firm providing logistics for other companies rebuilding Iraq.

In 1995, after having tried to sell our flat for several years, we finally persuaded a builder to accept the flat as a deposit for a new four-bedroom detached house on a new development, on the outskirts of Norwich. At first the house seemed very pleasant but crowded. There were seven of us, of three generations, living together and it was not working. Joan and I went away for a holiday and, when we returned our two daughters had been house hunting. They had found a house, only about three hundred yards from our present home, with a self-contained annex. The annex had, apparently been built for a widow, recently bereaved. It was small but, with the addition of a small conservatory, we thought we could live there. Helen and Frank bought the property and we have lived here ever since. Entertaining visitors is out of the question in our annex but, fortunately, Helen allows us to use her dining-room if we wish.

Since we have been in this situation Joan and I have managed to get away for, usually two holidays per year. So far we have been to the Algarve three times and Croatia once by road – yes, I drove all the way. We also visited Cyprus, Tunisia, Croatia and Malta, all by air. We have met many people who gave us a different outlook on life and lots of places we never thought we could see. In short we have had a good life and hope to carry on living it to the full.

~ End ~

Epilogue

We have all lived in this same house now for some fourteen years and are still on speaking terms! After our last trip to Croatia, by car, Joan seemed to be ailing. She had very little energy and, occasionally, complained of stomach pains. Our local doctors did their best to give her some ease and referred her to the Department of Medicine for the Elderly at the Norfolk and Norwich Hospital. Successive tests produced little improvement until she was admitted to the hospital towards the end of July 2007. She would be subjected to various tests throughout the week and sent home for the weekends, no doubt to ease the work of the nurses. At the beginning of August she was finally admitted and diagnosed as suffering from Pancreatic Cancer. The Pancreas is situated in the abdomen, close to the liver amid some rather complex 'plumbing'. It is extremely difficult to deal with but a young and very confident surgeon assured me they could tackle Joan's problem.

"We are doing it all the time," he said. "It's our job!"

An emergency operation was planned and took place on 31st July 2007. At first it seemed the operation had been completely successful but she started to deteriorate six days later. She suffered increasing abdominal pain and became very jaundiced. She was taken to the theatre for an emergency laparotomy on 7th August at about 5pm but arrested in the anaesthetic room and subsequently died.

The girls and I were completely devastated. We had come to the hospital on a routine visit only to be told that our darling wife and mother was dead.

The senior surgeon was most sympathetic and very curious to discover what had gone wrong. He, very tactfully, asked our permission to carry out a limited post-mortem examination. We agreed and another doctor carried out the procedures.

An old friend of ours, a retired surgeon from one of the larger London hospitals, told me, "It was a very courageous man who attempted to carry out the operation."

When all these procedures were completed, a cremation was arranged, followed by interment at the Garden of Remembrance at Horsham St Faith, north of Norwich.

When life settled down, somewhat, I took myself off on a journey Round The World, with stops in Australia, to visit my brother Richard and his family; then to Tasmania to visit one of Richard's daughters and her family; next to New Zealand to see a friend who was at Halton with me and our paths crossed several times afterwards. My final stop was at Seattle in America to visit my eldest granddaughter and her husband. It was a long and sometimes tiring journey taking some eleven weeks in all, but it was well worth the effort and expense.

Since that time I have lived my life as fully as I have been able. I tried being a member of Over 60's Clubs but finally gave them up; not quite what I was looking for. I have joined a group of ex-Brats who live in this area. There are about twenty of us altogether and about a dozen of us meet, every Tuesday, at about 10 o'clock in a local café. After cups of coffee and a résumé of the previous week's happenings, we split into two groups, the fit and the not-so-fit, to walk along a disused railway track. One group covers about three miles and the other about six miles then back to the café at twelve for lunch and more nattering.

From time to time we may visit Air Museums or other places of interest and, about twice a year, we arrange visits to nearby restaurants for a meal, to which wives and guests are invited. I have also renewed contact with one or two friends from our times in France. In particular, I have made contact with Roma, the widow of another doctor friend from Canebières. We are very good friends, although we live more than 200 miles apart.

Incidentally, Roma was the only person outside my family who read this book pre-publication. She persuaded me that it was worth publication. Time will tell...

Joan & I, attending our daughter's wedding.

Former Brats reunion.